Our Autistic Lives

Personal Accounts from Autistic Adults
Around the World Aged 20 to 70+

Edited by Alex Ratcliffe

First published in 2020
by Jessica Kingsley Publishers
73 Collier Street
London N1 9BE, UK
and
400 Market Street, Suite 400
Philadelphia, PA 19106, USA

www.jkp.com

Library of Congress Cataloging in Publication Data
A CIP catalog record for this book is available from the Library of Congress

British Library Cataloguing in Publication Data
A CIP catalogue record for this book is available from the British Library

ISBN 978 1 78592 560 3
eISBN 978 1 78450 953 8

Printed and bound in the United States of America

OUR AUTISTIC LIVES

of related interest

Trauma, Stigma, and Autism
Developing Resilience and
Loosening the Grip of Shame
Gordon Gates
ISBN 978 1 78592 203 9
eISBN 978 1 78450 477 9

**An Adult with an
Autism Diagnosis**
A Guide for the Newly Diagnosed
Gillan Drew
ISBN 978 1 78592 246 6
eISBN 978 1 78450 530 1

**Bittersweet on the
Autism Spectrum**
*Edited by Luke Beardon,
PhD, and Dean Worton*
ISBN 978 1 78592 207 7
eISBN 978 1 78450 485 4

**Autism Spectrum Disorder
in Mid and Later Life**
Edited by Scott D. Wright, PhD
ISBN 978 1 84905 772 1
eISBN 978 1 78450 037 5

Camouflage
The Hidden Lives of
Autistic Women
Dr Sarah Bargiela
Illustrated by Sophie Standing
ISBN 978 1 78592 566 5
eISBN 978 1 78592 667 9

Spectrum Women
Walking to the Beat of Autism
*Edited by Barb Cook and
Dr Michelle Garnett*
Foreword by Lisa Morgan
ISBN 978 1 78592 434 7
eISBN 978 1 78450 806 7

**Older Adults and Autism
Spectrum Conditions**
An Introduction and Guide
Wenn Lawson
Foreword by Carol Povey
ISBN 978 1 84905 961 9
eISBN 978 0 85700 813 8

**Very Late Diagnosis of
Asperger Syndrome (Autism
Spectrum Disorder)**
How Seeking a Diagnosis in
Adulthood Can Change Your Life
Philip Wylie
ISBN 978 1 84905 433 1
eISBN 978 0 85700 778 0

For Peter, Abbie, Rod, Marina, Andrew, Helen and Ellie.

Contents

OUR 60S

OUR 70S AND BEYOND

Acknowledgements

I'd like to say thank you to the autistic population (i.e. the experts) for believing in this book's ability to reduce isolation amongst autistic adults.

Thank you in particular to those who have contributed a personal account, for taking the time to share your thoughts and experiences with me and the wider world. Thank you for meeting me in person and online, for taking part in video and phone calls, and for filling in my (often lengthy) templates and questionnaires.

For every person who has contributed, there are many more who have given me their time, their views and their knowledge. Thank you to each and every one of you for making this book a reality.

Introduction

The autistic community makes up approximately 1% of the world's population. Many countries report a higher figure, including the USA at 2.2% and Japan at 2.7%. These percentages are from studies conducted post-2004 and many involved only children. They don't take into account those diagnosed as adults, particularly those who have been able to 'cope' and therefore haven't been diagnosed until later in life. The true percentages are even higher when you include those who are self-diagnosed or not yet officially diagnosed, such as me.

I want to point out that I'm not an expert on autism and that this book isn't about explaining autism or putting my own views across. Instead, it's a book about sharing views and experiences from a wide variety of individuals who happen to be autistic. It's a book that I wish I'd read many years ago.

It was whilst looking for such a book that I realised it was yet to exist and that the number of books containing shared accounts greatly diminishes as the age of the writer(s) increases. Although older citizens may not have obtained a diagnosis until relatively recently, these citizens still exist, as do their peers without a diagnosis. I believe that in failing to acknowledge the older generations, we are effectively failing to acknowledge a significant proportion of society. The term 'autism' was first described back in the 1920s, yet it wasn't until 1980 (when some of the contributors in this book were already in their 40s) that it started being used as an official diagnosis, separate from schizophrenia. Even then it was still labelled 'infantile' autism and was seen purely as an impairment, not a difference.

The number of people being diagnosed now is rising by up to 30% per country every year. This isn't because of an increase in autism; it is because of an increase in autism awareness. Autism awareness, however, does not mean autism acceptance. Although the world's understanding of autism has improved over time, statistics show that autism acceptance has a long way to go.

A study by the Karolinska Institute between 1987 and 2009[1] found that the average life expectancy for autistic individuals without a learning disability (so roughly 50%) was 54 years. This is 16 years below the neurotypical (non-autistic) average. Furthermore, a study by the CLASS clinic between 2004 and 2013[2] revealed that 66% of autistic adults had contemplated

---

1   Hirvikoski, T., Mittendorfer-Rutz, E. and Larsson, H. (2016) 'Premature mortality in autism spectrum disorder.' *British Journal of Psychiatry 208*, 3, 232–238. A study of 27,000 individuals with an autism spectrum disorder (6400 with an intellectual disability). This study compared those with an autism spectrum disorder with roughly 2,500,000 individuals without an autism spectrum disorder.

2   Cassidy, S., Bradley, P., Robinson, J., Allison, C., McHugh, M. and Baron-Cohen, S. (2014) 'Suicidal ideation and suicide plans or attempts in adults with Asperger's syndrome attending a specialist diagnostic clinic: A clinical cohort study.' *The Lancet: Psychiatry 1*, 2, 142–147. A study of 374 individuals who were newly diagnosed with Asperger's between 2004 and 2013.

suicide. This is 39% higher than the neurotypical population. A dominating risk factor of suicide is depression. It is important to point out that autism does not cause depression. But society's lack of understanding can. It can cause autistic people to become more vulnerable to feelings of loneliness, worthlessness and isolation. This book therefore aims to increase the acknowledgement of this segment of society, particularly those in their 50s and beyond. It aims in some small way to reduce those statistics.

The personal accounts you are about to read come from across the generations and across the continents. You'll encounter a range of terms including ASD (autism spectrum disorder), AS (Asperger's syndrome), PDD (pervasive developmental disorder), HFA (high-functioning autism) and PDA (pathological demand avoidance). This is because an individual's particular diagnosis depends on the year and country in which diagnosis occurred. Whereas some countries, including the UK, tend to use the ICD (International Classification of Diseases) to form a foundation for diagnosis, many use the American DSM (*Diagnostic and Statistical Manual*). In 2018, the latest ICD (ICD-11) was published, to take effect from 2022. It runs more in line with the latest DSM (DSM-5) which no longer has Asperger's as a separate diagnosis. Because of the changes within these updated manuals, ASD is likely to become the most commonly given diagnostic term worldwide.

Terminology used also depends on personal preference and belief. For example, many autistic people do not like to add descriptions to the term 'autistic'. They don't want to be known as 'high-functioning' or 'severely autistic'. They don't want to be put in a hierarchy or spectrum, and they don't believe there should be a distinction between themselves and the rest of the autistic population.

I recognise that views on self-diagnosis are mixed. Although the majority of contributions are from those who are officially diagnosed, some are from those who are self-diagnosed. There are a variety of reasons for this, including the fact that in many countries knowledge and understanding of autism is still lacking. In other countries a diagnosis might not be financially viable, and even if it is gained, there may be no support that is easily accessible. This is often the case for older generations in particular who may have spent many decades 'masking' their autism in order to survive in society.

Of course, this book is a collection of accounts by autistic people who are able to put their views across. I'm very aware that many autistic people are unable to do this in a way that society recognises or understands. It has been this awareness that has made this introduction difficult to write. I don't want to romanticise autism, but I also don't want to paint it as a negative part of someone's identity. Because it's not. Whether someone is able to put their views about being autistic across is perhaps less important than whether society is able to listen. I believe that many of the feelings and views within these accounts are held not just by autistic people who are able to recognise them and express them, but by those who cannot do so in a way that society recognises. Whether an autistic individual has a learning disability or not, they're an important part of society. They always have been.

Our 2Os

Gideon-Sebastian

Advocate

I'm a pansexual trans-person. I came out as pan at 18 and trans a few years later. I grew up Catholic but became an atheist at 14. My family aren't too happy about my 'lifestyle choices'. I just ignore their views and correct them when they mess up my name and pronouns.

At 21 I did my research and self-diagnosed myself autistic. Up until then I'd always felt that I was either some sort of freak or losing my mind. Shortly after my self-diagnosis, I pressured my mother into letting me see an autism specialist to see if what I suspected was true. It took several months to get in to see the doctor and then an additional four appointments that spanned over another several months before I finally, at the age of 22, received the diagnosis of autism spectrum disorder.

Realizing I was autistic helped me tremendously. It gave me great insight into myself and gave me a concrete explanation for my strange behaviors. No longer do I feel like a failure for things that are out of my control.

I greatly prefer 'identity-first language'. My autism is a part of me; it's not an accessory to be added or removed at will.

It makes me who I am. It's my neurology. Saying 'person with autism' implies that the autism is somehow separate, that it can be taken out, or that it's temporary. I don't like the similarity in phrasing to things like 'I have a cold' or 'I have cancer'. Autism is a harmless difference in the brain, not a disease. I am autistic; it is not a negative attribute, it's a statement of fact. Autistic is something I am, not something I have.

I was a late talker. My mother says I didn't start speaking until I was three, but that once I started, I spoke normally and never stopped. From what she described, I've come to the realization that I must have had, at least briefly, some sort of impediment regarding certain sounds. Specifically, those with the *or* sound which I would pronounce as *air*. So morning was 'mair-ning', door was 'dair', four was 'fair'. Apparently, I would have arguments with my grandfather to shut the 'dair' and that I was 'fair' years old, while he would correct my pronunciation.

A lot of my verbal communication is scripting. I have a semi-functional collection of phrases to get me through the most common social scenarios. My mother has commented that I don't have a conversation so much as make statements, which makes sense if I'm scripting a lot.

The downside of scripting is that it's only useful for basic small talk and very common interactions. Anything more intensive than asking and responding about the weather or how I am today requires a thought-out response, which is unfortunate and can make my responses unusually slow. I'm sure my interactions get boring as well if I'm always saying the same responses. I do try to kind of alternate my phrases every once in a while, so that conversations with me aren't quite so monotonous, but I'm not sure how well I accomplish that.

My language is already odd; it's stiff and formal. My terminology is also a bit different from the typical person my age. I'm American but I've always been obsessed with anything British. Because of this I've picked up a bunch of British terminology which has worked its way into my scripts. I'm sure this makes me come across as even more odd as the typical American doesn't go around saying things like 'This needs to be put in the post' or 'Mind the lorry' or 'Would you like a chocolate digestive biscuit?'

At a very young age I noticed that other people didn't seem to have obsessions like I did. They didn't seem to get as fixated about things. It made me stand out a bit when I wouldn't stop talking about Roman mythology or homeless people, or whatever my interest at the time was. Finding out I was autistic and that this was normal for us really helped me to realize that my obsessions were OK, and I wasn't weird for having them.

For as long as I can remember I've had an obsession with one thing or another. Sometimes they are normal and age-appropriate (*Scooby Doo*, *Harry Potter*, the TV show *Lost*) and sometimes they aren't (homeless people, prosthetic limbs, my 55-year-old boss). They usually last a few years before they disappear, usually when there is nothing more to be learned on the subject or a new interest develops. Some of them are a bit more awkward than others, such as my homeless person fixation. My parents found this one endlessly annoying because apparently a nine-year-old who talks about nothing but homeless people is embarrassing.

Snape from *Harry Potter* has been my greatest and longest-lasting special interest. There's always unnoticed or additional information about him to go over. I currently have two secondary special interests: *The Lion Guard* (although I love all things Disney, *The Lion Guard* is most important right now) and the British foster care system.

I love collecting things relating to my special interests. My mother usually yells at me for this as she doesn't understand how much I need these things. I own a bunch of *Lion Guard* stuff which my mother says is immature but whatever. *The Lion King* was my favorite thing when I was a kid and I think it's great that Disney has brought it back for the next generation. I have a bunch of British fostering memoirs and I have a ton of Snape stuff, the best of which is a life-size cut-out of him which is totally awesome.

About a year before I was diagnosed, I was really struggling with trying to keep up the appearance of being normal. I genuinely felt like I was losing my grip on reality; I thought I was having a nervous breakdown. Things that had never bothered me before became such monumental tasks that I couldn't cope. I started having panic attacks/fainting spells at the drop of a hat. I started having instances where I couldn't even force myself to leave the house. I dropped out of classes, the quality of my work at my job decreased, and large amounts of time were either spent zoned out or hiding in the bathroom. I was working in a clothes store when I ended up in the fetal position under a rack of clothes, sobbing, in the middle of my shift. I'd started withdrawing into myself and fixating even more upon my then current special interest (which was quite inappropriately my boss). It all came to a head when I was fired for my increasingly erratic behavior. I figured the best solution was to go and stand in the busy road in front of the store and attempt to be run over. My boss pulled me out of the road (which certainly didn't help me to get over him) and I ended up spending some time in the mental ward of the hospital.

It wasn't until nearly two years later, when I'd received my diagnosis and done some research, that I realized what I'd been going through was autistic burnout. After 22 years of trying to blend in and act normal, I said, 'Screw this', and stopped trying to pass. Receiving my diagnosis made me realize that no matter how much I tried, I was never going to be normal. It was detrimental to my health to try to be normal and frankly it seemed like a waste of time. So I stopped trying. I'm generally much happier; it's working out quite well for me.

The diagnosis identified specific behaviors I'd been living with for years such as walking on my tiptoes. I tend to only do it now when I'm excited or stressed; it leaves my calves feeling tight afterwards.

I love stimming (carrying out self-stimulating repetitive behaviors). It's the best thing ever. I stim all the time in one way or another. Basically, I never stop moving; I'll bounce my legs or rock, or I might rotate my shoulders. I have a ten-gallon bucket full of stim toys – tangles, stress balls, puffer balls and spikey animals. Outside of rocking, chewing is my favorite stim. I will chew on nearly anything – except fabric, which I have a horrible sensory reaction to.

When I was little, I used to bite my nails and chew off the skin around my fingers until they bled. My fingers were always sore and horrible-looking. I finally managed to stop but I'm still prone to doing it if I'm stressed and not paying attention. I was so happy to learn that oral sensory seeking is a common autistic thing and that there are special safe things to chew on. Before I knew about them, though, like I said before, I used to chew on pretty much anything – metal, wood, plastic, paper. My favorites (which I do still chew on when I come across them) were the little plastic pieces that attach tags to clothes. It used to be great at work because we had entire strips of them just lying about that I could chew on. I used to get nervous or bored and pick other things up off the floor too. I'm sure it was horribly unsanitary. I've been told I have a distinctive look that I get when debating whether I should put something in my mouth. Now that I have some proper chew toys, though, my propensity to chew on random items has gone down.

My autism tends to make everything in life seem too loud. People talk loud and traffic is loud. It's all very annoying and distracting. The cinema is awful sound-wise; it's painfully loud. I've taken to bringing my earmuffs with me to help muffle the noise. Interestingly, I quite like loud self-controlled noise or music – I guess because I have the option to turn it down/off if it gets too much. I find fluorescent lights super irritating. They're ridiculously bright and they flicker and hum. To combat this, I often wear sunglasses in public buildings. They come with the bonus of blocking eye contact.

To cope with sensory overload when I'm out and about, I like to listen to a metronome or some ASMR (autonomous sensory meridian response) videos. When overstimulated at home, I hang out in my closet. It's under the stairs, and when I was little, I used to hide in there and pretend I was Harry Potter. I've turned it into a sort of mini sensory room. I put a small TV in there along with all my old Disney VHS tapes. Disney is still always a good way for me to decompress. I have a bunch of light-up things in there such as my fiber-optic fan light. There's also my box of kinetic sand and a bunch of stim toys. I've put a futon mattress and a ton of pillows, blankets and stuffed animals in there. It's so nice and soft and comfy – a good place to calm down. The sensory processing issues I have are, I suppose, both positive and negative. It sucks to have such strong aversions to things, but at the same time the sensory input is amazing. So maybe I'll never be able to prepare raw chicken by myself, but the joy I get from touching soft things and burrowing under my weighted blanket kind of makes up for it. It seems that neurotypicals don't get to experience things as intensely as we do. I think that's kind of sad.

Special interests are definitely a positive (provided they are something appropriate). It's so easy for me to absorb all the information about a special interest – like you can be an overnight expert on whatever you're into. It's pretty cool. I don't really think neurotypicals have the same ability to do that, at least not to the extent that autistic people do.

Izanagi

Passionista

What makes me truly happy is practicing Aikido. I call it the moving meditation. My dream was to go to Japan, live in a Buddhist temple and practice Aikido. But my father told me I had to get a degree in something.

I'm a white, cisgender, heterosexual man, born and bred in Mexico City. I live in an apartment with my mother and have a Scottish terrier called Roy. Looks-wise, I'm tall and thin with bright-coloured eyes. My hair starts straight but gets curlier the further it gets from my head. I would say I'm handsome, but I don't feel like it a lot of the time. I have three tattoos: the neurodiversity symbol, AikiŌkami (I've practiced Aikido for many years now) and Prajnaparamita (the perfection of the Buddha).

I've been a Buddhist since junior high school and I try to make the world a better place by sharing my happiness with other people and smiling at everyone I meet.

Most days I rise at 6.30, have breakfast, then walk to the station with my face mask on (I don't like breathing cigar smoke and pollution). I use headphones too; the music helps me feel less anxious and I like moving with the rhythm.

I also like stimming while I walk. I stim pretty much all of the time, whether happy or anxious. I stim with my tongue, so it's very discreet (I've done it since I was a child). I enjoy it a lot, but when I'm overly happy, I feel the need to flap my hands very hard and to rock back and forth! It's so relaxing. Once at the station, I take the Toreo destination bus to work. It's an hour-and-a-half journey so I try to catch up on some sleep. I work in neuroscience in a really big building on the eighth floor. I use the elevator to get there, responding to people, saying 'Excuse me' or 'Have a good day' as I go. I get to my workstation, say 'Hi' to my co-workers, sit down, take my notebook out with my pencil, get my headphones, auxiliary cable and thermos out. I then get up and go to the bathroom to wash my hands (I don't like dirty things, so I don't like touching anything more than necessary until I'm all clean). I dry my hands with a single sheet of paper and fill my thermos with water.

I then sit down at my desk and work, and work, and work. I work non-stop, only taking breaks to help co-workers with their work. I really enjoy my job and I really enjoy working in general and helping other people out; I don't really need to take breaks. I've noticed that other people often take time out to gossip, to tell a story or a joke, basically to socialize. I don't quite get it. I get easily distracted (especially by noise), so if I'm not using my headphones, I end up hearing every conversation around me and my head flies through solutions to their problems and interesting facts about things. Occasionally, though, I get up from my place and tell them a fact or thing in my head. Then I return to my work.

I think that being autistic has helped me with my job because I can come up with solutions outside of the box. And it's not that I consciously think about them; my brain just does it at the speed of light. Being autistic is who I am, and that is what makes me beautiful, I think.

After work I head home to eat and prepare for my college classes at the faculty of sciences, where I study to be an actuary from 5pm till 10pm. I try to relax a bit before going out to my classes because buses and trains can be very uncomfortable. I don't like being touched and that happens a lot on public transport.

I have GAD (generalised anxiety disorder) and it makes me worry about nearly impossible things; I always have to imagine the *worst* scenario that could happen. One of my psychiatrists, though, has taught me how to stop my train of thought and rationalize things to stop worrying about them. So I can now make my brain think about all the possible outcomes with their respective probabilities and seek to end my anxiety by letting myself know that everything is fine and nothing bad will happen.

Besides the GAD, most of the time I'm pretty happy and joyful; I laugh a lot about many things. I don't really get sarcasm and I'm the last one to get a joke, but I do get the joke and I always find it funny. Sometimes I laugh too hard (OK, most of the time) but I think that's part of me.

I don't keep my diagnosis to myself because I want to break the stigma surrounding not only autism but mental health in general. People often ask me for help with their problems, like anxiety. Or just because they want to feel better. I know I might encounter some bad-intentioned people, but I think the bigger picture is more important than myself.

I'm really happy right now with who I am and with what I've

achieved, but sometimes I feel more autistic than usual and wish I had more friends on the spectrum to relate to.

I've *never* been any good with social interactions and I really don't get when people flirt with me; I end up confusing everything. I also prefer girlfriends to boyfriends; I really don't understand males in general.

I've had two relationships in the past. The first was really short. I was so naive and felt so anxious all the time. When we held hands, mine were always sweaty and that made me *so* uncomfortable. She was my first kiss and I didn't really want to because I didn't know how to do it, when to do it, where to do it, why to do it and so on.

My second relationship lasted almost five years. I didn't really want to marry anyone but then she came along and changed my world. We ended up getting engaged. We had an amazing relationship, but it had some bad, bad moments. She was abusive, but I did love her, and I think she loved me.

She was my first sexual encounter. Our first time was in my house, in my bed, and I didn't really know what to do. It was really funny and really awkward. We used to have sex a *lot*, like every time we got alone. It was great sex, I think. I feel, though, like she wasn't a good kisser (my other girlfriend used to kiss better) and that made things less pleasurable. She used to think I was cheating on her. She'd say, 'Where did you learn that?' and 'How do you do *that?!*' but I wasn't. What I enjoyed the most was giving her oral sex, maybe because I have premature ejaculation (which made things really awkward for me; I'm pretty sure it stems from my hypersensitivity linked to my autism). She always reached climax; she didn't let me breathe sometimes.

When we broke up, I fell into a horrible depression. It was

Christmas time and I didn't want to do anything. I was hiding my true feelings from everyone around me. I didn't tell my family or friends any of what was going on and I ended up having suicidal thoughts and ideations every day. Eventually, I started going to a psychiatrist and a psychologist. That's when things started to get better.

I'm single right now. I don't want to get with anyone for a long time. I think my autism affected the second relationship. She wanted to go out more, go to parties, get drunk. She did that in Belgium a lot when we gave each other some time, basically when everything fucked up. Thinking about it now, I guess she was living the 'normal' 20s life.

I didn't think about having kids at all with my ex, but I've always enjoyed playing with them. All my family think I would be a great father. If I did have kids one day, I'd explain to them all about autism. I do it with everyone around me, so it's obvious I'd do it with them too.

As a kid myself, I used to lose everything and get easily distracted; this was because of my ADHD (attention deficit hyperactivity disorder). I was very cheerful, though, and I had a *huge* imagination. I became fixated at one point on robots and cooking. I used to watch a cooking channel for hours and hours on end; I wanted to study gastronomy.

I still like to think a lot about *everything* and I love finding patterns that connect things I've learned. Basically, everything fascinates me! My long-time interest is still Aikido (although I now combine it with medical science). Ultimately, I still want to live in Japan and practice Aikido; I have a dream to get to tenth dan...

Alex
Guard

I video-call Alex a little later than originally planned. He's sitting at the desk of his spaciously sized home office, looking nervous. The first thing he does is apologise. He explains it's his day off and he lost track of time making YouTube clips. My first thought is that he looks different to his photos. He has an athletic physique and chiselled features. His speech comes across as very considered, as though he is checking his sentences before sharing them.

I'm not supposed to be in my job with my condition. I work in security and I'm quite high up. On paper, I shouldn't have been able to even enrol in this line of work, let alone succeed.

Typically, my day starts at about 4.30am. I drive 40 minutes to work and spend about an hour and a half doing physical work outside. I really like it; it's very different from the desert I lived in for several years. It's nice to be back in an area that's similar to where I grew up. Here there are trees and grass, real grass. It's always wet so there's the lovely feeling of moisture in the air. The rest of the day I spend in my office.

A large chunk of my job involves writing reports. I find this very hard as I've never been great with vocabulary. I was brilliant at learning sign language, though, as there weren't any words involved. The thing is, I tend to see everything in images rather than words and sometimes I'll forget what the right word is. So I might be describing something, and I can get some of the words out through habit, but other words just won't come. I'll see the image, but I can't find the right word and I'll just be standing there, blank. So, for example, I'll know that what I'm describing is red in colour, but I'll forget what the word is for red.

Because of how I am, people tend not to like me. I think they find me vulgar or too outspoken. Sometimes I feel that it'd be different if I was able to tell people about my condition. I think they might treat me differently. If they knew about my autism, I think there'd be much less friction. They'd be able to understand that I might be going through difficulties and we'd get along better as a result.

There have been a couple of people at work who've hinted at it and whom I've trusted enough to open up to. I haven't specifically told them about my condition, but I have told them I have difficulties. They've asked me questions about how they can help me, how they can work with me. It's helped a lot. It's helped me progress in my career. And so I wish society understood a bit better about what autism is. That it's different for each person because it's a spectrum. I wish they understood that just because I have this condition, it doesn't mean I can't function and succeed in my job. Because I can. And at the same time maybe those who can't do a job like mine can do something else that I can't. I think there should be some kind of a test where you have to demonstrate your ability to do different tasks.

I'm very good at my job but, as I said before, if my work found out about my diagnosis, I'd lose my job. I'd lose everything.

I've found that as I go up the career ladder, I worry more and more about my condition and about people finding out. I worry that they'll realise I've had it for a long time. I've also noticed that my ability to articulate my thoughts is going downhill. My speech patterns seem to be deteriorating and I'm increasingly unable to find the right words. It's a big concern. I try to look after myself, push myself into doing different things that I know are supposed to be good for me. So, for example, I've been trying to get over my lack of social interaction by making YouTube videos. I don't show my face in my videos and I have a fake name. I think it's doing me good; better than shutting myself away from the world which I've tended to do in the past.

I try not to get too stressed, but my job brings it on. How I am at home also doesn't help. I've been with my partner now for about nine years, married for five. She's been with me through the whole Asperger's thing. It's definitely been very difficult and there's definitely been some very dark times. Lots of fighting and periods without communication. I'm not a sociable person and she finds this very hard. We'll go to separate rooms, one of us to the living room, the other to the office. It's not unusual to go for about a week without speaking to each other.

I worry that all the stress in my life, at home and at work, might lead to Alzheimer's. It really scares me. Maybe not tomorrow, but at an early age. I worry about not being able to interact socially, verbally, or even at all. The fear of that has always been there – not being able to function independently, having some kind of a breakdown.

Aurora

Gamer

I work random shifts, so there's no such thing as a typical day. As soon as I wake, I set my alarm for an hour before I need to leave. I get dressed, go downstairs for a cigarette, let the dog out. I make the dog's breakfast (a delightful mix of raw meat and dry food), then sit down with a cup of tea until I need to leave.

My work revolves around supporting adults with autism in every aspect of their lives. It's a combination of office work and managing a team of staff. It works for me. I understand the need for routines and consistency, and I enjoy the non-neurotypical interaction (neurotypical being a term often used to describe people who are not autistic). Work is well aware of my diagnosis, but people that don't know me well tend to not believe it. Those that know me well can see it, though. My diagnosis helps a lot at work. It helps me support each individual because I understand their needs.

The only downside of my job is that shifts can last for up to 36 hours. I don't struggle with the number of hours, but I do struggle with the 'sleeping-in' duties that have to happen during shifts of this length. Sleeping in a different bed is hard. Without my weighted blanket, I often don't nod off at all.

Whatever the length of the shift I've just completed, the first thing I do on getting home is walk the dog. Or have a break and then walk the dog. Occasionally, I'm not able to get a break or walk the dog because my mum wants me to do something else straight away. If this happens, I tend to become overwhelmed and have a meltdown. This usually involves me falling into a bad mood, swearing and sometimes shouting. Once I've calmed myself down, I'll play on the Xbox, have dinner, watch TV in bed; wait till I fall asleep. For someone working random shifts, I didn't think routine was that important to me, but scrutinising my day like this makes me realise it is.

Unfortunately, there isn't much that makes me truly happy. I suffer with anxiety, especially in social situations. I also get migraines which I presume are due to the anxiety. When I am very stressed, I get very sensitive to touch. It can become so extreme that anything touching me hurts. I have to move around constantly until the feeling goes. The soles of my feet if I'm standing, legs if I'm sitting, my arms if they're even so much as gently resting on something. I use a lot of weighted therapy to calm myself down. Again, my weighted blanket really helps, as does chewing.

Most of the time I feel that I'm 'just coping' with everything; that I'm expending a lot of energy just about managing to fit in. I have interests, but I tend to become completely obsessed with them, to the extent that nothing else matters. Then I forget about them and move on to the next thing. I currently enjoy art and gaming; my current obsession is the Xbox game *Overwatch*.

I'm very anxious about my future. I'm at that age where I want to live on my own, away from my family, yet I also want to remain close enough for their support if I need it. I've been looking for my own place and I've seen a few nice ones, but

I haven't made the leap just yet. It'll be a huge change. At the moment I'm still worrying about managing money, being unable to sleep, doing things by myself. The one good thing, though, is that when I do move, my dog will be coming with me. That'll make it a lot easier.

I think I've found looking for a house especially difficult because I'm on my own. I don't have a desire to date or live with anyone either. I identify as asexual. Having ASD (autism spectrum disorder) as a diagnosis has been a huge help in me learning about myself and realising that there might be a link between my diagnosis and my sexuality.

I know a lot of people with autism and Asperger's, and I guess this is what has truly helped me to accept, understand and even get my diagnosis. All of us are so unique and have completely different routines and interests, likes and dislikes. All of us bring something different to the world and, quite frankly, I'm proud to be autistic.

Giles

Traveller

From experience, the rest of the world doesn't see me as a person, more as a thing. I don't believe in an afterlife, but I'd like to believe it exists. I don't want there to just be this, then death, then nothing.

I was diagnosed with mild autism in high school. Apparently, I was aware of it from a young age. I can't remember feeling aware back then, but I'm very aware of it now. Particularly how it affects my behaviours. My mum did her best when I was growing up. My older siblings didn't understand, though, and so they didn't treat me too well.

During school I was the one person that everyone seemed to target. Teachers did their best. Their best just happened to be the bare minimum. If I could give my younger self any advice, it would be that people are horrible. Get ready to spend a lot of time by yourself.

I currently live with my mum and younger sister. I don't really come into contact with anyone else. If I go out, it's usually by myself. People tend not to talk to me, but if they do, I end the conversation as quickly as possible. Until it ends, I feel quite tense.

My autism means that I can't stand people touching me

either. It's just something that makes me feel really uncomfortable. One good thing about my diagnosis, though, is that it lets me approach situations and problems without emotion. I find this very helpful. It's the reason I wouldn't ever choose to remove my autism.

I identify as asexual. In the future I'd like to have a relationship with someone; I just don't see it working for me right now. I'm not in the best mental state. The last time I checked with the doctor, he told me I was going through a mild bout of depression. That bout's still with me today.

Until I get talking to someone and find out who they really are, the world seems kind of empty. Unfortunately, if I'm in a group of more than two people, I regress into myself and am unable to talk. It's always been the case. I once tried to connect with a local group of people with Asperger's and autism, but I didn't feel like I fitted in. I do have a few friends, though.

They understand and respect who I am.

My passion in life is travel, I recently went overseas to America. I'd been once before, travelling around Texas, but I hadn't seen as much as I'd wanted to. This time I went for a month by myself. I stayed in B&Bs along the way, ended up spending half of the time in Los Angeles. Nice people in Los Angeles, but I wasn't prepared for their traffic. It was really bad; there was just so much of it. But I coped OK. It was whilst I was there that I made the discovery that food can make me instantaneously happy.

I'd like to go to Japan now; the culture really appeals to me. I'll stay in B&Bs like I did in America. I'm looking for work at the moment, though – data entry, admin, that kind of thing. Japan therefore won't be for a few years. But I'll get there. America was my biggest achievement in life so far. Japan will be my next.

Aiden
Musician

M ost days I tend to wake up at about 9am. I roll over, switch on my laptop and check my Facebook messages. I wish my important friends a good morning and step out of bed. Once downstairs, I proceed to greet my dog Alfie, my cat Minnie, my parrot Bella, and my budgie Joey. Bella usually whistles a random assortment of notes at me, tapping her beak on the side of the cage. My dog wags his tail in circles with a toy in his mouth, and I ruffle up his fur. My cat just looks at me like I'm a terrible person, and my budgie just tries to bite me because he has a Napoleon complex. They all say hello in their own unique ways and it's something I adore about these animals.

Greetings done, I down the last of my coffee and jump in the shower, hitting the power button of my desktop PC on the way past. It's always a Britpop playlist on Spotify, as it's always 1997 in my head. I hoover up and reload the dishwasher, because I'm obligated to, check my emails on my PC, and apply for more jobs as I'm currently unemployed. I make some instant noodles once I get hungry enough, and then go for a walk into town to kill some time. I just generally look around some clothes shops, game shops, and then walk the long way home. Autumn is my favourite season, and I love the colour of the world, red and brown everywhere. I usually listen to Nirvana's *MTV Unplugged* album, recorded in New York in 1994, when I'm out walking, and I think about everything during this time. Being young and unemployed does make you feel down. Your entire outlook on life changes for the worse and your confidence takes a nosedive. I was brought up to pay my way. I enjoy working, I enjoy feeling tired after a full day's shift. When I lack that structure, I feel like I'm sponging off the rest of society.

I'm currently trying to build a career out of my passion for technology. I find it all so engaging, and I love messing about with computers, whether that be building new ones or repairing ones that already exist.

I find job interviews very challenging, but things like night-clubs don't bother me that much anymore. After a couple of beers, I'll talk to anyone. I particularly enjoy meeting people who are just as sarcastic and dream just as much as I do. I'm a slight extrovert and I firmly believe that the stereotype of all people with Asperger's being hermits who prefer to be alone is just that, a stereotype. I appreciate that communication can be difficult, but all of us are fundamentally the same. We want connections to form, and all that takes is a 'How are you?' and a smile. If you're a good person, you pick up people as you go along. As for romance, I think I suck at being a good boyfriend, but I try my best. I don't think I look too bad and I can make people laugh. Women seem to appreciate a good sense of hu-mour and I think I have one.

I'm not really close with anyone else who has a diagnosis of Asperger's or high-functioning autism. I think seeing myself mirrored back to me would make me feel a tad uncomfortable. Saying that, I have had a few thoughts about one or two people I know. As far as I'm concerned, though, I don't really care what they're diagnosed with as long as they're decent people.

Ultimately, I do not care what anyone else thinks of me. I will stand up for my loved ones. I would take a bullet for any of them because I know they would do the same for me. I'm just a normal guy with morals and values coincidental to the place I grew up in and the people who have hurt me in the past. I have flaws. I am not perfect. Neurotypical population? What's one of those? Being around social media groups dedicated to Asperger's has taught me about an 'us versus them' school of thinking. I don't understand why people are so driven to divide. It also seems that there are many people who can't handle differences of opinion, people who make sweeping statements about huge numbers of people. They'll try to tell you what Asperger's is, when it's actually different for each individual. If you mention that you don't agree with them, you can bet that they'll try to bend you round to their way of thinking. It seems there are people who will preach on and on about inclusivity but will put themselves into boxes just to belong. Therefore, they'll blame the neurotypicals for everything. Nope. Sorry. Take responsibility for yourself and stop blaming others who aren't carbon copies of you. I love everybody as brothers and sisters. Everybody is worth something to me.

The best way to describe how I experience Asperger's is as white noise. This white noise stops bits of information getting through to my brain. When I'm working, it can make communication very difficult as it means I often misunderstand instructions.

Reflecting upon my experiences like this makes me realise how far I've come. I was a typical autistic kid growing up. I had a few sensory issues and I was not very coordinated. I bumped into things a lot. I could never understand jokes either. Social expectations didn't make much sense – all these rules without real reason or explanation. I remember at primary school, during assembly time in the hall, being coerced into singing Christian hymns. The teachers would either stand or sit around the edges of the hall and look bored, and we'd have to collectively mumble our way through these words being projected on the screen. It always seemed pointless to me. Once I started reading books, slightly Orwellian in design, I was turned off Christianity for life. I have also never had any feelings of allegiance to my birth country. I don't feel patriotic feelings about this rock floating in the ocean.

I was diagnosed as a kid, so it didn't mean much to me at the time. I was more interested in playing with my toy cars and running around in circles. Looking back, though, it confirms why I appeared so advanced to my parents and nursery school teachers but struggled with everyday basic tasks such as tying my shoelaces.

As I grew up, the other kids noticed I was different. This was their cue to bully me, right up until I left high school. A lot of self-hatred, a lot of depression and attempts at self-harm. I was withdrawn; I cried a lot. Most teachers didn't seem to care and those that did were unable to solve my issues. My parents were my only coping mechanism. I had anger issues because of the repressed frustration. These feelings haven't just magically disappeared. They're still there. They're the reason my self-esteem isn't great. If I could, I'd say to my younger self,

'You've put up with more in your childhood than most people have to put up with in their entire lives. Don't just sit there and take it. Stand up for yourself. You're talented and your parents love you for who you are.'

Travis

Father

I've always been a sucker for the clash and bang of rock and metal music. It soothes me. As does the sound of thunder. I love the scent of the humid air before and after a storm, the smell of when it rains after a long hot day. I don't like the sounds of the tornado sirens, but I do like to hear the heavy winds whistling by while I'm hiding in the basement.

My current set-up? I have an orange kitty and his name is Cheeto. And two sons. I rent a room in a trailer with some other people. I enjoy fixing computers, pretty much fixing anything I can.

A typical day starts with Cheetoh letting me know he wants to go out. I like cold mornings, frost covering everything in sight, the air crisp and refreshing. I step outside for a morning smoke, then get ready for the day ahead. When it's cold, I warm up the car and head off to my place of work.

Getting there in the morning and switching the lights on, the kitchen is bare and the restaurant is empty. It's my second home. I'm in control and I feel safe there. Cooking makes me happy, very much so. Having a new challenge to overcome, finally achieving those goals; it's an amazingly satisfying experience.

Anyway, I begin my opening routines of prepping necessary ingredients. While I work, I make sure to keep everything clean and organized, everything in its right place.

Sometimes, as I'm prepping, the boss's son comes into the shop to handle the cash. He never acknowledges me. It's awkward. Being ignored like that makes me either withdraw or feel aggressive. I know you don't have to acknowledge strangers, but with people you know, like at work, it's different. You have to make an effort. At work I really do make an effort. I become a different person; I attempt to be friendly by saying hi to everyone. I have my role and I know who to be and how to behave. I wouldn't say that dealing with people is something I enjoy, but my people skills have been praised by my bosses past and present.

When there's company get-togethers, though, I find myself out of place. I'd rather be with strangers. I seclude myself and seek out an excuse to leave. I don't enjoy being forced to socialize or being required to be friendly. Given the choice, I prefer to keep myself to myself; I like my solitude too much.

I don't give any thought to what others think about me. I don't want other people's opinions to affect me. I am my own person. I don't make many friends, but the few I do make I consider very close. I've never made a point to mention my ASD to people. I am different and that's what people like about me.

I wasn't aware of my Asperger's until my first time being locked up. Once there, I had a psychological evaluation done. Turned out that when I was younger, the schools had their thoughts on my being different. I always learned differently; making friends was never easy. When someone would suggest that I become their friend, I'd become very guarded because of how the general population would ridicule me, tease me, bully me. For being a loner. For wanting to be alone. Not wanting to go on field trips. Not wanting to do after-school activities. I just wanted to be home where I felt safe and sound.

Peers were always hard to get along with. A time in school where the class was to go for a weekend camping trip was a very traumatic experience. I had no choice and was forced to go.

Teachers and persons older than me were always much easier to get along with. With them, I saw the world in a different light.

Growing up, I was always the odd one out. I was a single child with a single mother. I describe myself as only half white. I never knew my father; my mother said he died. She said he was Cuban, so I took that to heart. White on the outside, Hispanic on the inside. My brown eyes and brown hair reflect my father. My mother's blue eyes and blond hair did not pass to me.

My mother was with me when I first tried pot. Our set-up wasn't one I saw other kids having. We moved around a lot; I didn't really understand why. I was taught to always run away from danger, avoid confrontation, don't fight, don't talk back, don't argue. Do not disagree. Do as you're told.

We finally settled into a town during my first year of high school. A whole new territory; fun to say the least. First crush, first girlfriend, first fight. Growing up, finding my feet. I hadn't been allowed to say what was on my mind because it was often too logical, too direct, too blunt. If I did, people would see me as negative or downright rude. Suddenly, I started talking back to my mother, standing up for myself. My mother lost her control; she couldn't punish me anymore.

Fast-forward to my graduation, and to my first time being locked up. I'd stood up for myself but had had trouble censuring my words. Ultimately, I'd come across as disrespectful.

My mother disappeared when it happened; I guess she felt like a failure. I know I did (although I didn't feel any guilt). When I was in jail, I got into even more trouble. For dancing and laughing and singing. I was alone, secluded, locked up. And I still got in trouble, just for enjoying myself.

As well as the Asperger's, the prison psych labelled me with schizophrenic-affective disorder, gave me all sorts of medicines. Medicines that made me numb, medicines that made me sick. Medicines that took away my will to live. The last medicine I ever took from him was lithium. When I was released, I wasn't required to take medicines anymore, so I stopped. I found other methods to deal with my – what's the term? – ah yes, 'things that I do that are Aspi'.

I'm a very logical individual. Constantly wanting to know why, who, what, when, how and where. I've always enjoyed problem solving. Taking things apart, whether it's something tangible like a computer, or intangible like a person's actions or behavior. Why did they hate me so much? Why was I annoying? Why did I crave all the attention? Why did I think so much, so intensely? Why did I not give my brain time to rest?

My diagnosis of Asperger's goes some way to help me understand why I think like I do. I've learned everything that I know not by going to lectures or reading but by actively participating. I've always learned by doing.

Growing up, I found relationships challenging. My first girlfriend chose me over her boyfriend. He was my first fight. Onwards to my other relationships. Sex at school turned into sex at work, sex in public places, casual sex with no relationships. Again and again, females chose me over their boyfriends. Or just cheated on them with me; kept me a secret. My view

45

of relationships subsequently twisted. Lots of sneaking, lots of secrets.

I married but had an affair. She was married too. We'd known each other since we were 13; we had history way before maturity. Years passed separately, then ten years later I met her again. In the ten years, the spark of 13 had never left. Our affair lasted years. One time we had sex on the anniversary of my wedding, at a church we'd attended as school kids. Years later we admitted our affair; divorces happened, but feelings never left. My ex-wife is the mother of my two children and we are still as close and intimate as ever. My mistress and former 13 sweetheart has been enjoying her divorced life, going through boyfriend after boyfriend…

I've learned that love is a feeling; it's a choice of action. I feel love via adoration and I choose to love someone by my actions. Love is spectacular and mysterious. I never thought life could be this way. I've pretty much lost track of what I wanted to say or share now. Life goes on. Rock on. I love to sing, I love to dance. I love to cook, and I love to love.

Daisy

Observer

I've never been able to manage to keep more than one friend at a time. I think my biggest hurdle is that I can pick up tons of info about someone without paying much attention to them. So, when I do talk to them, it comes across as too obsessed or creepy. Alternatively, it makes people think too highly of themselves and they start ignoring me just to measure my interest. I don't like to play mind games, so I only end up keeping the ones who think I'm merely being thoughtful or nice; the ones who proceed to return the same interest I give them. I wish people would spend one-tenth of the time I try to understand them on trying to understand me.

I'm 20 years old and from Egypt. I'm tall, incredibly skinny. With long unkempt hair, big golden eyes and a pointy chin. I don't really know how to dress; I just know I've never liked jeans. For better or worse, and for whatever reason, people are jarred by my appearance.

I moved around a lot when I was a kid, but I never managed to absorb any of the local cultures or dialects. Currently, I'm staying with my mom and older sister in a new city outside of Cairo. I'm here to be near university. Many people buy real estate here as an investment, but it seems like nobody ever lives in it; there are barely any shops or activities. I appreciate the quiet environment, though. It helps me control my sensory input. I have fairly stereotypical autistic sensitivities, except perhaps for picky eating; I barely have an appetite at all. I use several apps to keep track of daily activities, such as exercising, eating and showering. I also keep a detailed list of university assignments and their deadlines; I rarely get anything done without planning it.

I've had many special interests over the years, including digital art, photography, videogames, films, languages and psychology. I've always been interested in how and why people think. Probably because it differs so much from how I think. I like to understand people simply by listening and observing, not interfering. Like a biologist researching another species, I can't seem to learn anything when I'm part of the experiment.

I've always known how to excel academically. This doesn't mean, though, that university has been a pleasant experience. I picked the most neurotypical, most socially driven course anyone can imagine. Because I went with the intention of making lots of friends. I ended up having a meltdown on the first day because it was too sunny, and I got lost. I just didn't know it was called a meltdown back then.

I spent the next three years accidentally confirming things that I already knew, and that everyone else knew, but had always denied knowing. I'm book smart, but not socially competent. I'll never be one of those popular, desirable, well-dressed people everyone is trying to emulate. I'll never have a clique of friends to gossip and hang out with. I'll never pass a typical interview.

These 'quirks' I have are actually autistic traits, and I will never be normal. Not because I don't try to be, but because I will never be perceived as normal. People like to think that they stand above the crowd, that nobody understands them, that they are the main characters in their own movies, and that this makes them special. But if being different is such a good thing, why are we treated so poorly for it? And why do people go to ridiculous lengths to prove that they are part of a group? My musings, honesty and quirks don't actually hurt anyone, but they're extremely unwanted in a society that doesn't even let you have your own religious, societal or political beliefs. It's easiest just to stay quiet.

Anyway, how am I supposed to explain to people that I have what they think is a severe neurological disorder? That I was never diagnosed because I'm a girl with a supposedly high IQ, and that Egyptian doctors are poorly educated on the matter to begin with? Recently, I used the very few skills I've learned at university to make a short film about it. Most of the other students still don't get it, but people who don't get it were never my audience. I merely wanted to share my thoughts with other people like me, whether they knew they were like me or not.

Our 30s

Laura

Police Officer

I became a police officer three years ago having spent 14 years in the military. The police training was very hard (privately, medically and socially). I got a shoulder injury during my year at the police academy, had it operated on after graduating. My physiotherapist had a son with autism. Her mother and her sister also worked with autistic children and whilst talking to her one day she suddenly mentioned she suspected me of being autistic. I was in therapy at the time (still am) so I mentioned this to my psychologist. She said she'd thought about it too, but just didn't want to be as direct as my physiotherapist. We talked a lot about it during our subsequent sessions. She explained everything to me, what it means to have autism and why she thought I might be autistic. So, after ten months, I decided to do the test.

Getting a diagnosis made life easier for me and my husband. He understands me even better now. We've been together over 15 years, married for nine. There's a 20-year age gap between us. We met in the army where he'd worked his entire life. He retired last year. Now he's a full-time house man. He does all the shopping and cooking and practically all the cleaning and washing. We live in a three-bedroom house in a city suburb. We have a small garden in which I created an oasis for birds, bees and insects.

I'm always up by six on weekdays. Once at work, I start the day by greeting my colleagues. There are two in particular who I really like. We have a morning coffee together before I turn on my computer and daylight desk lamp, and get ready to start the day's work.

Around 10am someone brings a bucket of soup from the kitchen. At midday I eat my sandwiches whilst still working (I prefer to take a walk outside during my lunch hour).

After two months within my current post, I decided to tell my boss about being autistic. There were some miscommunications between myself and colleagues, and I didn't want to keep 'the mask' on any longer. I wasn't sleeping well because of it.

Since opening up, my whole life has changed enormously. I feel appreciated for who I am and what I do. My boss sees my capabilities better than I see them myself. She's willing to give me all the chances I need. I'm always welcome to talk to her; she has me give her a regular update about how I'm coping. She's trying to give me the work and the environment that's best for me. She knows I cope extremely well in surroundings where I know what to do, and where I can do it at my tempo, without people looking over my shoulder. She knows I can cope with deadlines and that I'm very skilled at delivering a good job at high speed.

Not everyone at work knows about autism or knows that I have it. Some people just think I'm a bit of a weird one, but in general they all like me. There's one colleague whose children have autism and she decided to do the tests herself. She's the only one I know who has autism. I stop working between four and five and head home to my husband. If there are no activities planned, we eat shortly after I get in. Afterwards I take a shower (every two days) and put on my home clothes. Sometimes we play a board game; sometimes we watch a movie. I often try to do some crochet and fill in my bullet journal. Most importantly, I enjoy relaxing in the company of our three cats.

Once every two weeks I have a therapy session in the evening and starting from next week there will be a weekly workshop too. I also have a weekly music lesson on the French horn which I started playing when I was 21. I try to practise my music every day, but that's just a dream. I've thought of going for a music master's, but there are already too many musicians and I don't have the natural talent required to be a professional musician. I need my teacher/mentor to help me unravel the music. I can read my score perfectly, but I don't always find the feelings within the piece.

Over the weekend my husband and I try to relax in bed for a bit whilst listening to the radio. I like to cuddle with him and sleep/wake whilst lying in his armpit. We often do some shopping Saturday morning and I try to do all the washing my husband hasn't got round to. Ironing clothes is for Sunday morning whilst I call my mum for a weekly chat. The rest of our time is filled with hobbies such as crocheting, painting miniature figures, listening to audiobooks.

We usually watch movies on weekend evenings, whilst having a beer or a whisky. We have a sexual relationship but I'm not the biggest fan of kissing (too wet). Roughly once a week (usually at the weekend) we have sex with orgasms and all. When my husband physically needs it, I also help him manually. I'm almost never in a position that I really need to have sex physically or mentally. It's not that I don't like orgasms; I just don't mind not having them.

I sometimes struggle to understand social conventions. Other people's reactions tell me when I've acted strangely or said something that isn't quite right. I'm always trying to fit in, but ever since I got my diagnosis, I'm looking to do it without losing myself. I'm constantly surprised at how the neurotypical population react to things; I find the differences between us fascinating.

I don't really like socialising, shaking hands and the obligatory nonsense talks. I find it difficult to see the difference between a friendship and a working relationship. As soon as I like someone, and we have common interests, I consider that person a friend. Because I know I'm having difficulties seeing the difference and seeing boundaries, I usually ask those people what I am to them. I explain the situation and ask them to tell me if I cross the line. I've never had negative reactions to my honesty. People appreciate it and they understand me more. They learn to be careful when using words/phrases because I tend to take a lot of what they say literally. I've reached a point where I ask what they mean until it's clear.

Just before getting diagnosed, I had what my psychologist refers to as an autistic burnout. Life was just too hard, and I was just too tired to go on. I wanted but at the same time didn't want to die. I just wanted to be left alone and to rest. I'm off the antidepressants now, though, and I'm happy. Happy with my work, my relationship and myself. The diagnosis has changed my life and I've had only positive reactions when I've told people about it. I could still do with a bit more self-esteem. But I'm getting there.

Katie

Blogger

It seems like it's very inclusive in the West; people talk about it more often. Autism isn't really spoken of in Asia, especially not here in the Philippines. Down's syndrome is, but not autism. I hope that this book will encourage others who live in countries where it isn't really discussed to be more open about it and to feel at peace with themselves.

I'm a freelance writer, a proud geek, an avid reader and an audiophile. I'm petite with olive skin and smooth black hair that refuses to be curled.

I live at home with my parents in a gated and quiet subdivision. Our house is three stories high, and we have a pool. My entire family of seven lives here. Plus my dog, the household help and two caregivers for my bedridden grandmother. It's a very quiet neighborhood in the metro south. Much quieter than in the north of the city. Down here everyone turns in pretty early.

First thing each morning I wash my face and start doing my Korean skincare routine. I then start writing and creating graphics for my blog. Afternoons are spent doing social media work, freelance writing for clients, etc. Sometimes I go to mass at noon; sometimes I go in the evening.

I've always been worried about my non-existent love life. I want to get married, but I'm scared of not being accepted by my future partner because of being autistic. I'm also worried that any future kids might end up on the spectrum. That doesn't stop me wanting to be a mom, though. I'd just be very much on the alert to see if they exhibited any signs of autism. If they did, I'd like to be able to do early intervention. That's what I'd have wanted, if we'd known when I was younger.

I found out about being autistic by accident because of my bipolar aunt. She was staying with us and blurted it out one day as a kind of insult. It felt like she was blaming my autism for what she saw as the negative part of my character; as if she was implying that being autistic can only be a negative thing.

I'm part of a group of young Filipino autistic adults. We met online and have now met up in person. Most of them would rather remain anonymous because they're of working age and afraid of losing their jobs. I'm also not as open about being autistic as I could be. I did try to come out of the proverbial closet twice but even though I explained, my friends didn't understand what it meant. I guess the attitude of the Filipino people is just not as open yet as it should be. Those that are more accepting consist mainly of educators or family members who have relatives with autism. Most of the Filipinos that talk about autism online are parents of autistic children. There are programs for these kids. But nothing as yet for the adults.

I have a blog that aims to improve autism acceptance. Starting it was scary as it was so personal, but the feedback has been amazingly positive. People have been supporting me, telling me that it's something that's needed and that it really does help. The whole process helps me too. I look at things more objectively now, it allows me to be more reflective about myself.

Growing up, I used to be fixated on the fall of the Roman Empire. And then there was a passion for the American Revolution. I now have a fondness for Philippine history; I love going to heritage sites with the Spanish-era houses.

I've always had a big interest in trivia. I read encyclopedias and *National Geographic* magazines and I used to have these two books called *The Big Book of Questions and Answers I* and *II*. I'd study them as if they were Bibles. I'm also a whiz with Disney trivia, a typical 90s kid still.

I've always loved television, stories and watching movies. My interest in pop culture, especially science fiction, was cultivated thanks to my dad who let me watch *Star Trek: The Next Generation* growing up. I then found my grandmother's Betamax tapes of the *Star Wars* original trilogy...

After high school I took a degree in Theater Arts. I'm proud that I graduated more quickly than any of my siblings. I currently have a web series idea that I'd like to work on, a modern take on a Filipino classic. I can't wait to actually do it, to see my ideas become reality.

In my spare time I love going to fan conventions and taking part in cosplay. The last three I've been to as characters from *Doctor Who* – a gender-bent Eleventh Doctor, Osgood and Sarah Jane Smith. I'll be cosplaying next month as *Ruby Rose* from *RWBY*. I already have the wig, corset and red cloth to make a cape. I've always loved dressing up in costume. I become someone else and can be more confident in meeting new people. At the same time, I can be myself in liking these things. As I'm surrounded by like-minded people, people who feel the same way.

Naomi

Spiritualist

I have a very cold house. It's not fit for human habitation. I always make sure I look a million dollars, so no one can tell the state of the place I call home. I have two heaters, but I can't use them concurrently; they use too much electricity and flip the breaker switch. I alternate them therefore, depending on which side of the house I'm currently in. It's ridiculous.

My blinds are too thin and let.in too much light at night. It makes sleep hard. I have hypersensitivity to heat and light, and my situation aggravates it. I have difficulty regulating body temperature and this exacerbates my dyspraxia symptoms.

Due to my allergies, breakfast is rarely a hoot. Sorghum biscuits with water, caffeine-free tea, an apple; my staple diet.

Since moving to England, I've had over 20 people asking me if I'm autistic. I think it's because autism is more widely recognised here than where I used to live. I currently have an appointment for an assessment. I've come to realise how neatly my entire life seems to conform into the categorical boxes for ASD. As well as the autism, I also identify as white and straight. I think non-heterosexual orientations and even non-binary identities are also forms of neurodivergence, yet I've never heard anyone refer to them as such.

Politically, I identify as centre right. I find that hard to say, though, as my peer group is overwhelmingly far left. I'm very pro-life. I didn't start rigidly identifying myself as this until I discovered that my mother had had an abortion after my brother was born. It happened a few months before I was conceived. She was bullied into it by my father. The only reason I was born was because they were too poor to send my mother abroad to have another abortion (it's still illegal in the country of my birth). I therefore became their second-born child. Everything was fine and none of us suffered. My father looks back on family life with nostalgia now, something he told me he thought he'd never do as a 'forward-thinking man'. I think that both of my parents are autistic, but they don't entertain the idea. I'm pretty sure that my brother is the only neurotypical person in our family. I'm glad that my parents had a family. It's taught me that two people on the spectrum can make it work long-term.

My employment history is sketchy. My last job was as a healthcare receptionist, but I couldn't handle the multitasking and the pressure. People had a tendency to lie over the phone and it would stress me out. Sometimes they weren't lying but I thought they were; that got me into trouble too. I was supposed to work a phone, a computer, pen and paper, face to face – all at the same time. Discerning people's intentions made me feel low and out of the loop. It was no better with my co-workers. Nobody at the time (including myself) knew what was wrong with me.

In terms of the future, I'm nervous. Despite the hardships, though, I wouldn't change a thing about my life. Spiritualism helps me; it's a big part of who I am. Communicating with the spirit realm, it's very real for me. I'm blessed with a life of synchronicity and have been assured that my current circumstances are temporary. I don't think I would have such 'qi sensitivity' (a conscious intelligence of the energy and power within the body) without the autism.

My current goals are to start my own business, write a book, start a new relationship. I'm afraid of doing any proper dating at the moment, though, in case he wonders why I don't bring him back to mine. I'm looking like a million dollars, remember.

I've had a number of relationships in the past; I've even been married. My ex-husband was also autistic. I was drawn to him because of it, but it didn't work out because of it. We had a long-distance relationship; we only met in person right before our wedding. I had no idea we were both autistic, but because of the energetic empathy I had, I felt he was somehow like me. I was just out of high school and communication was fraught with difficulties. It was hard to express how his comments about me hurt deeply. It was even harder to discuss moving to another country. After our wedding, he didn't kiss me again for seven years due to 'sensory issues'. He just didn't like it. He didn't talk to me much either, but he did occasionally talk *at* me. He could type reams in an email to me, but face to face he'd shut down. This was something, of course, that I didn't experience until after we got married. The sex was infrequent and austere. He said he felt used, and it was true, I was using him. Because any other form of intimacy was never initiated or even liked by him. So I never tried a more holistic approach. The disconnect was a gaping hole that never got mended. He's separated now, with a child by another woman. That marriage was even shorter. I bet he still doesn't realise he's autistic. I bet he also still has his fifty-plus farm fowl collection living with him in his backyard.

Avi

Composer

I'm gay, Jewish, musically gifted, hyperlexic and learning disabled. I am basically Hitler's Worst Nightmare!

I have dark brown hair, glasses and a beard. I'm a little over-weight but I'm comfortable with my body. I'm also single and I've never been in a long-term relationship. I don't ever want to have children, and I'm proud to stand up for other people who feel the same way. I can barely take care of myself as it is.

I currently live with my parents as I find it hard to manage practical tasks such as cleaning, doing laundry, organization in general. With their financial support, I'm able to work part-time as a library assistant. I'm saving, building a small nest-egg while working on my creative pursuits. I know this can't continue forever. I hope I'll be able to find a supportive-living center in the future when my parents can't help any more.

As a child, I battled internally to make sense of the extreme discrepancy between my strengths and weaknesses. It upset my parents when I'd come home from school terrified and dejected at the daily homophobic bullying and eventual physical assault. They were perplexed when I started doing poorly in subjects like algebra. They couldn't reconcile the same son's level of intelligence with the one who had perfect musical pitch, the one who composed original music in his head and transcribed it onto sheet music, but who, to this day, cannot ride a bike, catch a ball or tie his shoelaces together. I agonize over how my life would have turned out if I had received an Asperger's diagnosis back then.

As it was, I had to leave two colleges, each time due to mental breakdowns. I couldn't handle the stress of living away from home. I constantly blame myself to this day for not being able to keep up with the demands and expectations of the neurotypical world. Back then I simply believed I was an incompetent slacker, undisciplined and wilfully incapable, but no different from any of my peers who failed to live up to their potential.

I identify as a man with Asperger's syndrome because Asperger's is a better fit according to my uneven cognitive profile, and the length and degree that I passed for normal during my childhood. I believe I am typical of many of the 'atypical' adults of my generation. Too high-functioning and hyperverbal to receive an autism diagnosis, too gifted and studious in subjects of great interest for our learning disabilities to be recognized, too intelligent on the surface for our executive dysfunctions to be addressed.

I used to argue with my father, who is a clinical psychologist, that an official diagnosis is an absolute necessity if one wants to become a published author or a public figure with credibility in the field of autism advocacy. Without a college degree, who would take someone like me seriously? One of my fears is to be accused of 'faking' it. Having an autism diagnosis in adulthood allows me to be secure in my identity and to take responsibility for my own needs. It also allows me to forgive my teachers, my parents, my mentors and myself for not knowing why I was suffering so long. My diagnosis is not a crutch or an excuse. It's like the comfort of a weighted blanket when I get exhausted or overwhelmed. It's a map of my life in reverse that does not tell me where my future lies or where I'm going, but it lets me see how I got here.

When I'm not working, I enjoy doing whatever I like. I can read as many books as I want, keep as many computer tabs open as I see fit on my screen. I can relax and just be. I don't have to justify or explain my idiosyncrasies and habits to anyone.

More and more autistics are opening up about their status as adults, and libraries have a critical role to play in meeting our needs. I am extraordinarily blessed to have a job that is fulfilling. I enjoy working with members of the public, helping people find the resources they need. Because of my desire to heal from the failures of my past, I also really want to help the next generation of young adults on the spectrum. For years I've envisioned a library outreach program specifically designed for adults like me. Very soon, through my efforts and my manager's blessing, our library system will have its first ever Community Autism Expo! We'll be inviting students on the spectrum from local high schools and a dozen autism service-providers to come along. They'll be able to share the services and resources that exist in our community for young people who've just finished high school. It breaks my heart to read the struggles of these young adults who either don't have steady employment or are terrified of disclosing their autism diagnosis to their employer for fear of it being terminated. I've been open about having Asperger's syndrome at my work for several years. Half a dozen managers later, I'm still going strong.

I think that identifying as autistic when you present or pass as normal, highly verbal or high-functioning Asperger's is a radical choice. Identifying with people all across the spectrum allows us to politically support each other regardless of functioning level, level of assisted living or how verbal we were in childhood.

I'm constantly inspired by people who push back against fear and find creative ways of relating to those who are different from them – people who turn their dreams into reality and make the most of life despite the hardships that they've been through.

It's at this point I ask Avi about his greatest achievement in life. He directs me to 'read a few articles about my musical' and moves on to my next question about his views on this book.

This book should have been published decades ago. Popular TV shows tend to showcase autistic people as young, white, male protagonists from middle-class families. The public has yet to see the diverse voices from older adults on the spectrum. The very notion of what constitutes 'adulthood' is challenged by the stories and perspectives of autistic people as we age, because we often don't develop in the expected ways or in the expected time frame like neurotypical people do.

Later I read reviews of Avi's musical about young adults with Asperger's. Every review is positive; every analysis heaps praise on what's been created. I learn of his published essays, his professional music career as a freelance composer, and his honourable mention for a well-known poetry prize. I find out that in 2016 he even received his first academic citation in a published research paper on the American novelist Philip Roth.

Annie

Teacher

I went into a large cosmetic shop recently. There were four different speakers covering the shop floor. All of them were playing different pieces of music, all of them playing it very loud. When I asked someone about it, they said because some of the stands were concessions, they could play whatever they liked. I had to leave empty-handed as I just couldn't cope with the sensory overload. It's strange: by law, many public buildings have a ramp in case someone has an accessibility need, yet they tend to ignore how their lights, sounds and smells can negatively affect people's access. I think that should change. After all, it's not just autistic people who get sensory overload.

I've never understood emotions. In a dictionary definition sense, I can tell you what they are, but I can't identify them. They're too overwhelming and I often just cry. I cry because I'm not sure what I'm feeling. The only emotion I recognise is frustration. For everything else I can only tell you a colour I feel. I am blue, or pink, or light green, or olive green. I use shades of light and dark to explain if it is a weak or intense emotion. I also struggle with feelings of hunger and thirst, so I often get to the point of feeling faint or sick before I realise what it is I need. Basically, my understanding of sensory feelings, whether internal or external, is weak. This means that I'm easily confused and exhausted.

I've been a teacher across different schools now for ten years. Every morning I get up early, get dressed and then change my outfit six or seven times to find the one that is 'right'. The transformation to 'adult' begins once again.

My morning commute is filled with music from films (*Gladiator*, *Pan's Labyrinth*, etc.). And then, at exactly 7.45 my mum calls. Not for any reason other than a 'Hey, how are you?' kind of chat. I don't know if she knows it, but it grounds me for the day. Hers is usually the first voice I hear on a morning. We just chat about anything, moan that it is Monday, look forward to the end of the day (we both work in schools), talk about what we are doing that night. I love it and I love her for it!

My working day is based on routine. I know what time things happen, when I get a break, what I have to do. I've become so used to masking my difficulties that no one can see when I'm struggling. No one can see when I want to scream and cry and lash out because I can't take any more. The end of the school day is when I mentally crash. I go back to being non-verbal and I can literally feel the speed of my brain slow down. The longer I don't speak, the calmer I become and the easier I find it to function as an adult.

My life has been spent in teaching. I've taught across the board. Primary, secondary, college, mainstream and special needs. When I started, I was always trying to do the job how I thought I saw others do it, but I found it harder than most to know when or how to switch off. I'd often do 13-hour days, five days a week, before working at the weekends too. It was never-ending, but no one told me of the expectations outside of a lesson. I was labelled a hard worker, someone you could depend on, someone who would always go above and beyond (beyond what, though, I never knew). As a result, I often moved about, both in jobs and areas, because I couldn't work out how to balance work with my own things that made me happy. I put it down to the job being wrong each time, and I took people's advice to move on.

One day in my last job, a colleague asked me, 'Do you think teaching is right for you?' I realised for the first time that people saw me as the issue. Me being the thing that was wrong. Not the job or the school or the staff I work with, but me. I was the thing that needed to change. I knew and still know that my heart is right in teaching, but I've never had support for coping emotionally and mentally at work. I've asked for help, but because I always look as if I can cope, people have always felt I don't need it. No one has ever shown me how to balance work and life; no one has shown me how to cope socially with other staff. I've always been a great teacher in the classroom, but as soon as the bell goes, I have to be a sociable adult and that's hard.

Before I got my diagnosis, medical professionals (from GP to a lead psychiatric consultant) told me that I was mentally unwell. They said this for 20 years, that I had a mental illness of some sort. From bipolar, to dissociative identity, to borderline personality disorder. They said my only hope of help was an admission to hospital, but that that would only happen if I did something to warrant it. Over the years I was given a total of 13 different types of medication and was eventually admitted to a psychiatric ward for three weeks. I ended up pleading for a referral to an autism specialist. It took just a matter of months to receive my diagnosis. It's changed my life. I finally feel a positive sense of identity.

My view now on Asperger's is that it's just a form of autism. I'm glad it's no longer given a separate label. When it is, people tend to think of you as this super-brainy, socially blunt, weird, geek character who must be good at maths or science. Although I am a bit of a geek (and proud of it), that's about as far as it goes. Stereotypes for autism don't help either. If you meet one autistic person, you have done exactly that. You've met one. I have never met someone like me in my entire life; that being said, I've also never met another openly autistic adult face to face.

I've had one long-term relationship of four years and have been single now for six. I wish I could find someone to share my life with, but as soon as I bring up autism and being autistic, they back off. I can see the reaction on their face and I know I won't hear from them again. I'm not incapable of love and I understand love. I just don't show it in the way that others do. I want to find love, and someone to spend my life with. I want marriage and a family. All the things other non-autistic people want. I've had to resort to online dating and I've now tried various sites and apps. The same things happen, though. If I mention autism in general, it starts a conversation. If I mention I'm autistic, even if it's 20 messages in, it'll all go quiet. I've had friends say not to mention it, but why shouldn't I? Why should I not be honest about something that impacts on every aspect of my life?

I think the rest of the world views me either as someone who is fingers in ears, screaming, rocking back and forth, making noises not words...or as Rain Man. I happen to think I'm a bit of both. I flap my hands, but I don't spin. I have echolalia (repetition of speech that I've heard), but I can make eye contact (albeit painfully). I struggle daily in social situations but I'm super-clever in others. I'm not a puzzle, I'm not missing something. I'm just me. A whole person. I'm able to do all the things a neurotypical person can do, just maybe not in the same way. I don't need someone by my side every second of every day, but I do need someone to help me some of the time. I need acceptance and support and friendship. I don't need these things because I'm autistic. I need them because everyone does.

James

Introvert

I'm employed by a mail-opening business. It's a mundane job that follows a predictable routine. Predictability can feel comfortable for autistic people, but it can get boring. I feel as if I'm stuck in a rut. Confined to a dull, tedious environment. Unfortunately, I just don't feel like I'd be sufficiently good enough at any other job. I tried two others before this one. Didn't find true job satisfaction in them either. Ultimately, any work is better than being unemployed. It's just lucky I don't really *care* what the work is. My faith, my family and my personal interests are far more important to me.

Getting an official diagnosis of Asperger's felt like I could be sure I wasn't stupid. It helped me to see that my communication difficulties were not my fault. My parents were very relieved to hear that they were not to blame for my strange habits.

It seems to me that interacting with people in social situations is like playing some sort of game that I don't enjoy. A game for which I don't know the rules. Most other people do, but only on a natural, subconscious level, and they won't explain the rules to me since they presume that I already know them.

Through practical experience, and trial and error, I have partially learned how to play, yet the rules still seem to change when I'm least expecting it. Playing the game for long periods of time leaves me mentally exhausted. I need time alone to recharge my social batteries. Any advice I get about socialising goes something like 'Just be yourself. But make sure you act the same as everyone else.' A contradiction if ever there was one!

Although I had a supportive upbringing with kind and loving parents, my childhood was unhappy. At school I was bullied by teachers and classmates. I was the weak, lonely wimp who got picked on because bullies could tell I was an easy target. Four years of psychological abuse damaged my self-esteem and gave me emotional baggage that still lingers, even today. I lost count of how many times teachers told me to try harder, without explaining exactly what I was doing wrong, or what specific things I should do to improve. If you are repeatedly told that you are stupid, by various people, eventually you start to believe it. I hear it is common for autistic people to be treated like this.

Metaphors were absolutely foreign to me as a boy. When teachers said, 'Pull your socks up', I would pull up my trouser leg, look at my foot, and say, 'But my socks are already up.' I think the teachers thought I was being sarcastic, when actually I was genuinely confused.

Having sensory issues is common for autistic people. I would describe it as having my internal volume turned up too high. It's uncomfortable to watch television if the screen's brightness, contrast or volume is on what I perceive as an extreme setting. Everything becomes too bright, too vividly colourful, too noisy. Imagine experiencing that constantly, in real life, but with all kinds of sensory input: temperature, tastes, smells, light, colours, sound, physical pain, any tactile sensation. It's as though the brain exaggerates the sensory input. So, to an autistic person, the world can seem louder, smellier, more intense, more painful. If we are in a situation in which we can't reduce or control the sensory input that we perceive as extreme, it can be overwhelming. Personally, when the weather is sunny, I'm always the first person to complain that the sun is too bright. During the summer I never go anywhere without my sunglasses. I can't stand fire alarms or car alarms going off near me. They are agonising to me. I suppose, though, that everybody finds them annoying in some way.

Some people don't want to identify as autistic because they don't want the stigma of there being 'something wrong with them'. I don't believe that's the best way of looking at it. If something like this really is part of who you are, you should accept it as part of your identity; it's who you're meant to be, so express it. Just as gay people celebrate their sexuality by way of the 'gay pride' movement, I feel we should feel free to celebrate our unusual neurology as part of who we are. The 'autistic pride' movement.

I think that the rest of the world typically perceives autism in a very negative way – as a form of brain damage, or unwanted condition. The view that autism is caused by vaccines still persists. It distorts people's perception of what autism is and how it affects our brains. The subject of person-first and identity-first language provokes much debate. Person-first language means referring to us as 'people with autism', and identity-first language means saying 'autistic person'. One objection to person-first language is that it makes autism seem like an illness. Person with cancer, person with AIDS...

person with autism. When the pattern of language is the same, it gives the impression that they're all the same kind of thing – pathologies or diseases that should be curable. It's a false, misleading way of thinking about it. It ultimately leads to prejudice, discrimination and ignorance, the mindset of 'let's cure this awful disease called autism'.

A far more positive angle is to see autism as an integral aspect of 'who the person is', not 'what the person has'. Gender, race, sexuality, age and religion are all parts of people's identity. If I used person-first language consistently, it'd be like saying 'I'm a person with Britishness and heterosexuality'. Nobody talks like that. I am British. I am heterosexual. With neurological differences, the same logic applies. I don't have autism. I am autistic. Big difference. You can't separate autism from the rest of me. I didn't get infected by it, and I don't suffer from it. There are positive and negative things about it, but, ultimately, being autistic is nether good nor bad. It's just a natural part of who I am. And I happen to like being me.

Nicki

Health Professional

I usually get woken by my two-year-old standing by my bed shouting, 'Mummy, up!' His four-year-old sister will be close behind. I take them to the living room, get them a drink, make myself a tea. Once they're settled, my husband takes over, and I get ready for work.

It's a 15-minute drive to the hospital and it's quiet when I arrive. The reception desks are still closed, visitors haven't arrived yet, just staff making their way to offices and wards. There's a strong smell of coffee, and the sound of computer keys tapping as people check emails and schedules. Once we're all ready, we meet up together, go through patient lists, plan for the day, make sure needs are being met as a team.

My job involves moving from patient to patient, assessing them, explaining what's happening. I set up plans with the other team members, make numerous phone calls, write reports, provide coaching to my colleagues, talk to families. Sometimes I stop for a break, sometimes I don't.

It's not long before the wards and the offices become quite overwhelming for me. So much noise and movement. People rushing around, multiple conversations happening at every moment and in every direction. The bright lights overhead and the computer screens glaring. The machines beeping, patients calling to staff and staff calling to each other. It can be hard to concentrate; it can be hard to filter out all that stimulation. There aren't any quiet places to go, nowhere that can act as a temporary refuge.

Home is a compact three-bedroom new-build in the suburbs. It isn't a refuge either. I pick the children up from day care moments after finishing work. It's a full assault on the senses. Loud and boisterous pre-schoolers. I gather up two bags, two coats, locate two sets of shoes, two sets of socks. My children are young and excitable; they talk non-stop. Once we get home, they race around, upturn boxes of toys, set all the noisy ones off simultaneously. It's chaos I can't control, so I just have to be happy. I make dinner, run a bath, get them ready for bed. They choose a story each and it's then that we have a calm moment, sitting in their bedroom with the lights turned low. I like the rhythm of children's books, a gentle few minutes, just the three of us.

My husband gets home shortly after they're asleep. By that time, I'm completely exhausted. I ask how his day was, talk for a moment; then we finish the evening with books or TV.

I didn't think my life would look like this. I never saw myself married or with children. It's more than I ever dreamed of, but it's also the hardest thing I've ever done. I'm constantly on the edge of burnout, but, looking back, I think I've spent most of my life on the edge. Thinking about it, at this point in time, my life is the best it's ever been. I'm loved, I'm safe, I'm valued.

As a child, I was the odd one out. I didn't know what to do

to fit in. I tried copying what the other girls did, but that didn't work. I tried copying what the adults did, but that didn't work either. I worked so hard, and got good marks for effort, but it wasn't matched by the marks for achievement. I was told to try harder, but that didn't make sense; I was trying as hard as I could.

I was bullied at school and neglected at home. My first recorded episode of self-harm was at nine years old. At 15 I found myself in a social worker's office, accompanied by a teacher. The reason was family violence.

By the age of 20 I was at university, depressed and having panic attacks every day. A tutor suggested that I talk to the student support services. They assessed me, sent me to an educational psychologist, told me I was dyslexic and autistic. Suddenly, everything made sense.

I decided to tell a couple of people about it. My university lecturer told me I'd never be able to be a health professional. My parents told me that 'psychologists will label anything'. A friend said that 'everyone is on the spectrum somewhere'. I felt their responses invalidated my new-found sense of self.

I proved my lecturer wrong in the end. However, during my first year of working I was nearly referred to my own team for medical care due to depression. I had to confide in my boss that I'd been diagnosed as autistic, and please could he ensure that my referral for help wasn't among the dozens that we went through at each triage meeting. He was kind and encouraging, kept my news confidential. I told my second manager too, but unfortunately he wasn't as supportive. I lost some confidence and he questioned my competence. Once again, I found myself sinking into a black hole of nothingness. Depression became my comfort zone; it was far easier to hide away from people than leave the house and have to face them. I didn't understand what I'd done wrong and I didn't understand how to fix it.

Despite all odds, I did, though. Now, more than a decade later, I have stability and confidence. I'm tired but I'm happy. Although I mask a lot at work, the mask slips away for my husband. He's very patient. We deliberately talk about all sorts of things so that we're not making assumptions about what the other might be thinking or feeling.

Every day I marvel at the social intelligence of my children who seem to innately understand things that I don't. I seek comfort in books and in snatched moments of peace with a scenic view. I love the sound of birdsong and I'm working on mindfulness to manage anxiety. I take joy in hearing my children laugh and when they climb onto my lap for a hug. I'm still learning how to be a good parent, still learning to be a good wife.

Skywalker

Writer

About 15 years ago, I found myself walking into the CLASS (Cambridge Lifespan Asperger Syndrome Service) clinic in a village near Cambridge. I sat anxiously in the office of Simon Baron-Cohen, world-famous autism researcher and psychopathologist. Sitting opposite me was the cousin of Sacha Baron-Cohen aka Ali G. I was awestruck. They only have the vaguest of resemblances, yet all I could see was a thick gold chain round Professor Baron-Cohen's neck with the golden letters AUTISM spelled out. The fact he wasn't actually wearing a necklace like that didn't stop me shouting out, 'IZ IT COZ I IZ ASPERGIC?' For shame. Catchphrases aren't my forte at the best of times, let alone to famous people's cousins. Funnily enough, I walked out of that office with a diagnosis.

I also now have a diagnosis of Meniere's disease. This means I get regular vertigo attacks. My hearing has been gradually deteriorating to the point where I now use hearing aids. The hearing loss confuses my brain because, as a part of my autism, I have auditory processing delay which means my brain is slow to recognise some sounds. I also have hyperacusis, which means that certain pitches are tremendously painful to hear.

As well as all this, I don't like to be touched by most people. It actually hurts me; I get a burning sensation on my body wherever the touch has occurred. I don't shake hands; I flinch away from people because the prospect of suffering so much pain is terrifying. Growing up, my grandfather was the only person who could touch me without it hurting. I would sit on the arm of his chair and polish his head (he was bald) whilst clambering all over him. Then he got ill and had to go into hospital. He spent six months in there and then ended up in an isolation ward where I wasn't allowed to visit. I couldn't even talk to him as it was before the days of mobile phones. He died, and I never got a chance to say goodbye, never got a chance to touch him again. I was physically and mentally all alone in the world.

Over time I've learnt that touch from those I truly love, or have loved – my wife, my children, my deceased grandfather – doesn't burn me. Love to me is all-encompassing; I hyper-focus on the person of my affection. I need to be near them, I need to be able to touch them frequently, and I'll never, ever betray or dishonour them.

I have three children and the oldest and youngest are autistic. The oldest knows he is autistic and is almost as knowledgeable as I am. I have high hopes that one day he'll be able to continue where I've left off and that he'll help make the world a better place. My middle boy is neurotypical and the most laid-back child on the planet. He understands what being autistic means as he and his brother are only a year apart. He's grown up witnessing his brother's meltdowns; he understands how things work. We're really careful to make sure he's not left out between two very demanding siblings. The youngest is four; she knows the word and understands what being autistic means, but she hasn't applied it to herself yet. It's important to me that they'll all grow up being who they want to be, for them to be comfortable enough in their own skins to be able to say, 'I'm autistic'. To be proud of it, without feeling the gaze of judgement or dismissal.

It's our youngest child who usually comes and crawls into bed with my wife and me at about half six each morning. She likes to pretend she's a cat, meowing very loudly for extended periods of time. On waking, I go from nothingness to a tsunami of senses: people talking, showering, tooth brushing, stomping around looking for school uniforms, arguing because there is only one TV and three children who all want to watch different things. I usually get the kids sorted while my wife gets ready. I'm inevitably faced with a barrage of indecision over who wants what for breakfast, culminating in them all having exactly the same thing they have every day. This precious time passes by in a blur of extreme noise and movement. The house visibly settles like a sigh when they leave for school.

I no longer work for anyone. I did for a long time, but the stresses involved led me to go through what is known as autistic burnout. A bit like a nervous breakdown, I was shut down for months. The result of years of masking and suppressing autistic traits, years of having to deal with societal pressures. Ask any autistic person why we tend to die so early, and they'll tell you that it's a combination of stress, anxiety and exhaustion from years of masking and hiding. Society kills us, and I fear that my time is short.

I run a marketing consultancy with my wife and I'm also a professional freelance autism advocacy writer and blogger. The majority of my life is spent writing, fighting for autistic rights on the internet and in the real world. When I'm not writing, I'm usually talking to someone on the phone or speaking to a group or at a conference. For anybody, that would take its toll, but for an autistic person it's exhausting. Talking to familiar people is painful enough, but at least with someone you know, you can start to learn and recognise patterns in their speech, you can tell by the noise they make when they suck in air that they're going to speak. Talking to someone new is terrifying.

I work hard to navigate the world with as little actual human contact as possible, whilst also trying to write as much as I can. My stand-out thoughts are usually empathetic ones. Contrary to damaging popular belief, autistic people *do* feel empathy. Due to the subject matter of the things I write, I get a lot of messages from parents of autistic children, desperate for help. It's harrowing reading some of them, heart-breaking. What makes it worse is that I have to fob most of them off with generic answers. I send them off to certain Facebook groups for support, because I literally haven't the capacity, emotionally or physically, to help them all.

After work I pick the kids up from school and spend a lovely half hour hearing about their day. Once home, they disappear off in three different directions, tablets tucked firmly under their arms, only to reappear when I call them for dinner.

Post-dinner is family time. We play cards or board games. There's usually a meltdown or two from my two autistic children, an assault of noise and then, once calm resumes, there's a lovely hour where we watch part of a film or an episode of *Doctor Who* (which my boys love), while my wife puts our little girl to bed.

Once the boys are also asleep, I tend to make dinner for

my wife and me – something fresh like pasta or a steak – and then it's the nicest part of the day, when we have a cuddle for an hour or so.

My wife tends to go to bed before me. I stay up and write for another hour, and then, at the thought of going to bed, executive dysfunction kicks in. My brain farts and stutters, I find myself uncontrollably rocking back and forth on my heels, and I get caught on the same thought, repeating it over and over again. I lose track of time until another hour's gone by.

I see people I suspect as autistic everywhere. There are a lot more of us than the world thinks, just undiagnosed. The professional world is often running to catch up with us.

Both of my grandmothers have been retrospectively diagnosed; my father was deemed un-diagnosable. According to his diagnostician, there was a spectrum for him somewhere; they just hadn't found it yet!

My eldest sister (I'm one of three) was diagnosed at the same time as me, and her son is autistic. My middle sister's husband was also diagnosed at the same time and they have two autistic sons.

I think the rest of the world generally sees us as a puzzle (hence that awful jigsaw piece everywhere). The neurotypical world really struggles to understand us. Society is like a machine; it runs smoothly when all the parts are in their component place and doing what they are supposed to do. Autistic people do not stay in our place or do what we're supposed to do; we are separate from what society deems 'normal', which is why there is the common urge to treat us and cure us and make autistic people act like neurotypical people.

I have reached a point in my life where I do not care how the world views me; I do not need validation from other people. If someone wants to be shocked because I don't do small talk, or stare because I stim in public, or think me rude because I don't look at them, well, that's their problem, not mine. I've spent too many years hurting myself in order to make neurotypicals feel better and comfortable. I think it's time we were afforded the same courtesy.

Despite what you might think, I have no ill feeling towards neurotypical people whatsoever. If I did, I wouldn't be married to one. I do hold ill feeling, though, towards those who seek to cure people of autism. Those that use dangerous chemicals or refuse their children vaccines because dying of measles is apparently better than being autistic. I've seen people do horrible things and say horrible things in the name of 'fixing' autistics, and I wish they'd stop.

I do wish that more neurotypical people, especially those in positions of power in politics and the medical and education professions, would listen to us. The majority of the community wants the removal of functioning labels and would like to be called autistic instead of 'having autism'. Little things that cost society nothing, but still it refuses us. It really likes to cling to its own labels. Society should listen to us in terms of how we want to live and be supported. Too often we are told what we need; we are rarely asked. The current culture is that the autism narrative is written by professionals; professionals decide what we need, professionals train other professionals, professionals apply the services, professionals pat each other on the back and tell each other what a good job they've done. Sometimes they bring in autistic people to validate what they are doing or saying, but it's usually only those who are never shown the other side of the argument. All we ask is to be properly involved in the conversation; it's our minds, bodies and souls after all.

My dream and goal and aim is for autistic acceptance. Not awareness, but acceptance. I would like one day for it to be understood that autistic brains are different to neurotypical brains and that there is nothing 'wrong' with that difference. We tend to exist more in our own heads. Some of us have the ability to build worlds inside our minds and spend time there, oblivious to the outside world. There is nothing the matter with us, we do not need to be fixed or cured. We're amazing, just like everyone else. Not bad, not good, just different.

Aline

Depressive

Since 2014 I've prayed every day for someone up there to be kind enough to end my life. I can't take it anymore. I don't think I'd be missed that much. I don't know that many people in the first place.

I'm a big girl to look at. Brown eyes, brown hair, pale white skin with freckles. I'm French, heterosexual and a believer in deism.

People who know me call me Wikipedia. Because I know a lot of useless facts about everything. I like to learn languages, but because I find it hard to talk with new people, I forget the words very quickly. I had a period where I loved wrestling, but I kinda lost it when I stopped having a TV at home. I like games, the ones you play around a table with everybody, because it's social. I like watching people play videogames, because there's a story involved. I used to love playing *Final Fantasy XIV*, but due to financial problems and a bug in my computer, I can't anymore. I wasn't good at it, but I still loved it anyway.

I've got an IQ of 136, but it doesn't mean much when I see my seven brothers and sisters all do better than me. My mom told me I learned how to read by myself when I was three, so they made me skip the last nursery year, and enter straight into first grade.

I was quite good there, didn't have to work hard, everything was easy to learn. I had trouble, though, with left and right – still do. For the first year I had eye trouble too, had to get eyedrops as the world would get blurry.

I used to want to be a vet. But as soon as I got to sixth grade, my scores began to drop drastically. I entered a private school for 'gifted' children but they didn't teach us anything about *how* to learn. So I began to have trouble with stress. In exams I'd freeze, my mind would go blank, numbers would change from a 5 to an 8, + would become %, and I would inevitably fail. My dad coped with it by moving me from one school to the next.

I never had any friends as a child. In high school, I was the 'listening, quiet one', the one people would talk to, always outside the friend circle. The one no one asks how they are, what they're interested in. I felt really lonely; I still do. I'd like to make friends, but I can't. Every time I try, I'm tagged as 'strange', 'scary' or 'overwhelming'.

Despite all this, I ended up in nursing school.

Once there, I met my ex-husband. I guess he was the first person who genuinely took an interest in me and talked to me as a person. He was the first one who waited for me to answer. He was the only good thing I had in nursing school, pretty much the first good thing in my life.

Not long after I started there, one of my brothers took his own life. I saw everyone devastated. My mom, my dad, my brothers and sisters, their wives and husbands. I felt sad but also awkward. It took me a long time to admit to myself that it

wasn't his death that made me sad. Rather, it was seeing everyone around me so low, seeing the huge void that he'd left. He
was so bright, so talkative, so intelligent, so fun. When people
visited our home, I'd lead them to him. Because he was so good
at talking, people would be happy just to listen. They'd forget all
about me, that I'd brought them there in the first place...

I stopped nursing school, worked here and there. Ended
up in a big telecom company in Paris, in charge of clients that
would call to terminate their plan and line. Every day, all day,
I'd hear people screaming and swearing. One day I had a panic
attack. Then a massive and continued headache, together with
blackouts, lots and lots of them. They became a regular oc-
currence. They'd happen after angry phone calls, in crowded
subways or outside under bright lights.

I went to see numerous doctors and specialists about it. Had
many tests and took a lot of medicine. Neuroleptics, antiepilep-
tics, anxiolytics, painkillers. At 27 years old, I was taking up to
63 pills a day. It wasn't doing me any good, so I left Paris and
went to Montpellier instead.

My husband had to stay behind to tie up the loose ends and
I came to realise whilst we were apart that I didn't miss him. I
liked him a lot, still do. But deep down I never saw him as a
husband. I didn't want to have children with him and, after
a while, with distance and reflection, I realised that he was a
great friend, even a bit of a father figure, but not a husband.
So I told him I wanted a divorce. It hurt him a lot at first, but I
guess right now he's better where he is. He's still in Paris with
a great new girlfriend and three kids. He's happy, they're happy,
everything's for the best.

When I moved, I started seeing a psychologist and at first

she told me she thought I was a sociopath. Then she said it was Asperger's. I'm currently waiting for an assessment. In France, it can be a long wait.

I have a new boyfriend now and three cats. I live in a tiny flat and each and every day is the same. I wake at five, feed the cats, make coffee for my boyfriend. We say our goodbyes and I go back to sleep, before waking again at eight. I try to walk to work because I want to lose weight, but often I take the bus.

I still work for that telecom enterprise, but my role's slightly different now. There are fewer angry customers to deal with. I've tried to talk about Asperger's to my manager, tried to have adaptations done to my workspace. It hasn't worked. She's said she doesn't want it to seem like she's doing anyone any favours...

I tried to tell my family about Asperger's too. My sisters were very kind and understanding about it. One of my brothers, though, refused to listen; instead, he told me every cliché going. 'You're not Rain Man. You just want to be in the limelight for once. Everyone is autistic, autism doesn't exist. You're not rolling on the floor in your own slime, therefore you're not autistic.' His views hurt me a lot. Because he should be more accommodating, what with him being a doctor and everything. And then there's my boyfriend. He listens but he then expects me to adjust, to change.

I don't know what I want in life anymore. Although I'd like to change jobs, I don't know what else I can do. I don't like the city I live in, but I don't know where else I'd go. Even though I'm in a relationship, I feel lonely. Also, I have lots of debt with my boyfriend, so we need to stay together to pay the bills.

My mom used to say that when I was younger, I didn't have any social barriers. That I was able to ask perfect strangers things, even when she or my brothers and sisters were too scared to. She used to say I was a free spirit. I'm shy and stuttering now; I no longer look people in the eye. I've changed so much over the years. I no longer understand the reason for living.

Our 40s

Jen

Author

I'm a man trapped inside a woman's body, but I don't feel that a sex change would be beneficial. My wife (who is not on the spectrum) is also a man trapped inside a woman's body. We get along well. I associate as gay and as an atheist. A gay female atheist, who's also an animal rights advocate.

I enjoy chatting on the phone to my young nephew, but I don't want kids and neither does my wife. We live in a three-bedroom house with our cats and our dog, Marcus. Marcus makes me very happy. After work he's always waiting to greet me with my wife, Lisa.

My wife and I co-write fiction. We're obsessed with it. A lot of my day-to-day thoughts tend to be about whatever story we're writing. It's sort of our escape from work and reality.

At the moment I work six days a week at two separate jobs. I get up at five each morning for the main one. It used to be retail, but I hated it. I now work a shift from seven till half three, Monday till Friday at a warehouse, and I love it. We're a hotel/motel, service industry manufacturer of room signs, easels in bathrooms, stuff like that. My job is to OK the proofs and make sure the products are ready to go before they're shipped out. It's repetitive and detail-orientated. And I'm good at it. I worry about losing this job, though, about not being able to find another. I don't interview well and, although competent, I rarely make it past the screening stage.

I hate most of my co-workers. I find them loud, lazy and living in their own little privileged worlds. My Asperger's helps because not many mistakes make it past me. I also work a Saturday shift at the supermarket. I have one friend there, but I think the rest of my co-workers across both jobs see me as someone who is a clean freak. Someone who is obsessive and who thrives on routine. Someone who is stubborn and has trouble with sarcasm. These views don't matter to me, though. I just think differently to other people. The neurotypical population seems chaotic in comparison.

As a child, I started talking at six months old. I could sing by the time I was a year old and I was reading at three. I hated school. I found children my age loud and I often wanted to play with them but didn't understand their games. I was a happy kid, but I had a lot of sensory issues. I liked routine, and when things didn't go according to plan, I'd have bad meltdowns. My parents just figured it was due to me being spoilt. People said that I was a jabberbox and I got in trouble in school a lot for bringing things in from home and not paying attention. I was overly smart and got very bored. I was tested in sixth grade and it was determined that I had college-level intelligence. Why my parents didn't just have me skip grades, I'll never know.

I'm proud that I was able to move out of my parent's house. Just moving out and being independent on my own before moving in with my wife. Just in general being able to set up doctor's appointments, paying bills and keeping my finances in order, being able to get myself to work on time. If I could go back in time, though, I'd let myself skip grades at school. I'd have pursued an early degree in biology, gone off to work with wolves. Wolves have always fascinated me.

When I was about 15, my father tried to commit suicide. Turns out he had an aneurysm about to burst. He eventually got the help he needed and went on to make a full recovery, but I didn't understand why everyone was making my mother cry and I got rather angry at them. I think having Asperger's made it much harder, because, without asking, I had no idea what others were feeling or why they were doing what they were doing.

Keith

Typist

When I was about three or four, one of my aunts bought me a Batman suit. It fitted me perfectly and I wore it all day, insisting that everyone call me Batman. I then refused to take it off. I slept with it, showered with it; my whole identity became Batman. The only way my mother could get me to remove it was when she convinced me that it was damaged and needed repairing. By that point I'd been living in it for a few months, so once she'd got it off, it went straight in the bin!

I had a similar thing with a toy called Grover from Sesame Street. From the age of six till eight, I had him with me all day every day. I used to treat him as if he was a person. In the end, on a cold day I sat him next to the heater and he caught fire. I cried for weeks.

Phone books, the *Guinness World Records*, encyclopaedias and dictionaries – as a child, I read them all cover to cover. By this point I'd received my diagnosis of autism. Aged ten, I was taken to the cemetery by my mother, to see my grandfather who'd recently died. I remember being fascinated with all of the cemetery plaques. I started putting them in date order, first by how old they were when they died, then what year they died, what year they were born, surname, first name, everything. I didn't have enough time to finish it, so after we went home, I went back there the next day after school and kept doing it. One of my great-aunts who lived near us saw me one day and asked who I was paying respects to and I said simply, 'Nobody, I'm counting.' She got really upset and told my mother. I never really understood why that was disrespectful. If anything, I thought I was treasuring their memories more by thinking of people I didn't know and wondering about their lives.

My mother wanted me to be gay, so I had homosexuality as the default. I came out as straight at 13. My father has always been a bit homophobic, so he never had an issue with it. For a long time, I considered getting a sex change operation to become a woman. It was kind of like after I recognised that I was definitely heterosexual; then the next step was whether I wanted to be a woman. I concluded that if it was fully reversible, then I'd try it out, but since it wasn't, then I'd never consider it.

I loved school but was bullied a lot. It's funny because I took most of the insults literally so didn't realise I was being teased, but then suddenly they'd hit me for no reason – apparently out of frustration at my not realising I was being teased. I was hit a lot and I learnt to run fast. I also learnt to pick kids up and throw them.

Apparently, my body language makes me look like the most dishonest person the world has ever seen. It's because I have a huge amount of trouble maintaining eye contact when speaking. I have to force myself to have any at all. I combat this by never lying about anything. I don't think anyone should ever lie in the first place, though. I don't think politicians should lie. I don't think lawyers should lie. I don't think we should have intelligence agencies if their main reason to exist is to lie to each other, and then to find out who is lying about what. Imagine a world without lies! It wouldn't resolve everything, but it'd be a whole lot easier to understand.

I currently work as a typist. It makes me very upset if I'm late, so I always make sure I'm early, talking to myself as I walk to the train, working out whatever I need to work out. My boss finds it weird when I call to say I'm late, when I'm actually ten minutes early. But that's late for me! Before, when I've had to catch two trains, I've got in an hour early just to be sure.

Every minute of my job is accounted for perfectly. There's a time limit on my typing, but I have my own rules. My own rules are much harsher than my boss's; I need to be the best in the workplace. In fact, if anyone has any information about anyone who used to work there, I have to be better than them too. If anyone ever beats me, even once, on anything at all, I get upset. I try not to tell anyone that, but I do.

The only difficulty I ever have in a job is hiding how good I am at it from my co-workers. If they find out, they will invariably try to get me fired. I've been fired from four out of my last five jobs because of my autism, and I've won all four court cases easily. Unfortunately, this makes it harder to find someone who'll hire me. It's like I'm supposed to be ashamed for being discriminated against. Yet I am not ashamed. I feel kind of proud of it. Winning court cases against big companies is a big deal, and I never had any lawyers help me (although the companies did...). I feel proud of that. But everyone tells me I should feel ashamed. I am supposed to feel horrible about it. But I don't.

Over the years my obsessions have helped me deal with problems in life. There was a time when I couldn't talk to anyone, but then I had an obsession about making friends and after that it was fine. I used to have a problem with talking to girls, but again I had an obsession and then it was fine. I have worked out how to deal with physical bullies and even cyber-bullies, and I am sure once I get an obsession about how to deal with workplace bullying, then I'll be fine with that too. It just hasn't happened yet.

I don't care if I'm late coming home from work. Sometimes I'll even take extra time on purpose; it helps to relieve some of the work-day stress. When I do get home, my wife is waiting for me, cooking. We used to try it with me cooking, but then we'd eat too late and she was never happy about that.

Eating dinner is our big deal for the day. It's our main time talking. Afterwards we each have 'me time'. My wife uses hers to watch her favourite TV show, *Neighbours*. Then we do the dishes and have 'quality time', which is one of three things: (1) watching a movie, (2) watching a TV show or (3) playing a computer game together on the Xbox. After that, the rest of the night is 'me time' for each of us, though sometimes we'll interrupt each other to show each other a funny joke or something. We rarely go to bed at the same time as neither of us can get to sleep if we do.

On weekends or holidays it's a bit different. We often go to a movie or shop together. I like shopping but in a different way to my wife. I 'search and destroy', whereas she likes to go to 15 different shops and still not buy anything. I cook every day on weekends to make up for during the week. I also help with any housework and do anything that she can't do like fixing whatever. I am not very good with the fixing, but I'm better at it than she is.

Sometimes I think that to diagnose autism you just need someone else who has autism. In my 42 years of life, I've only met three people who are clearly autistic, two of whom were married to each other. Sadly, they broke up soon after we became friends and it was awkward to stay in touch with either of them afterwards. I felt this really wonderful bond with both of them. It was kind of like going on holiday overseas and meeting someone who is from the same country as you.

The other autistic person I've met was a girl at work. We used to talk, both of us not stopping, yet we could simultaneously understand what the other was saying. People at work used to describe it as us having our own language. My wife got jealous of her, though, not understanding that the link wasn't sexual, that it was more like we were the same species. It was a special kind of bond, but there was nothing romantic about it. It was different.

I have a small handful of friends. It's not that I can't make friends; I just have a really high standard. I used to beg if a friend did something mean, begging them not to leave me, but nowadays I just cut them out of my life. Maybe if one day I can figure out who is going to betray me before it happens, then I can have more friends, but until then it's just not worth it. Despite this, I currently have two of them. Two female friends that my wife and I do things with occasionally. Unfortunately, my wife thinks one of them likes her, and the other one seems to like me, so it's a bit awkward.

Meeting new people is absolutely awful, especially within a party scenario. For example, if I go to a party with one person,

I will end up either clinging to that one person or sitting by myself all night long. One of the worst times was when I went on a date with someone I didn't know well. The date was at a party and they abandoned me early on; apparently, to them it wasn't a date at all.

I guess the last time I was in such a situation was when meeting my wife's extended family about six years ago. I just sat with my wife and pretended to be more affectionate than I really was, so now anytime I see them I have to be overly affectionate towards her, just because I was the first time they met me. My wife now complains, though, that I'm annoying, that I talk too much, that I over-share, that at times I'm really difficult.

When bad things happen, I tend to obsess over them for a really long time and there comes a point where I want to move on, but the obsession won't let me until it is over. I have people screaming at me to stop it, but there is no way to stop it. I just have to let it run its course, and even the worst obsessions still have a positive purpose, even if it is just about realising how to avoid such a horrible situation again.

When I was younger, I had a problem with women. I was attracted to both the good and the bad, but kept going for the bad ones, the ones who'd do crazy things. When I was 19, an ex-girlfriend took one of my shirts, cut it up to look like a person, attached it to the antenna of the car parked in my driveway and proceeded to set it on fire.

I have loved, and still do love, many of my exes. But there was always some reason we couldn't be together, some fatal flaw. I loved one girl who refused to have an argument with me, and after about 20 refusals we found we couldn't talk about anything at all, and the relationship became impossible.

Two of my exes had abortions and I still get sad sometimes that it didn't happen. My wife doesn't want children, although sometimes she says she does. We have a little cat. The cat was meant to be practice for a child.

One of my wife's stepbrothers has two children and sometimes I babysit them. They don't know that I have autism and it isn't relevant. They know I do things a bit differently to other people and they are OK with that. Sometimes I think that the label of autism is unhelpful. Maybe it's better to describe some of my differences rather than having a name that just confuses people. Then they can make up their own definition of what it really means.

John

Mechanic

I talk to John from the comfort of his van. It's his day off and he'd usually be out by now on his motorbike. He's wrapped up against the elements – woolly hat and multiple layers. His face is decorated with piercings and a beard. When he starts talking, I'm met with a broad Midlands accent. 'It's not really very nice around here,' he says. 'Too crowded. If you smile at people, they say, "What you lookin' at?" If you frown at them, they say, "Who you makin' faces at?" You don't know how to look at them. So, you try not to look at all.'

The way I see it, there's a lot of information out there when you look up 'child with autism'. When you look up 'parents with autism', you automatically get responses for 'parents of child with autism'. I'd like that to change.

I've got seven children altogether. Two are from earlier relationships; the rest have been with my wife. We've been happily married now for 14 years. I didn't know much about autism until recently, but now, barring my wife, I think we're all on the spectrum.

I was diagnosed with autistic spectrum disorder last year. To be honest, it didn't come as much of a surprise to my wife, but it did to me. She'd been on about it for years and I eventually went to get tested when I realised it might help our daughter. She's 11 now and was diagnosed at the same time. My wife had been saying for a while, 'There's just something not right; she's just like you, she's just like you!' And I'd say, 'Yeah, but what's wrong with that?' And she'd say, 'It's just not right, it's just not right.'

But it all seemed quite normal to me. I'm starting to realise it's not. Like inappropriate speaking, an example of which occurred when we went to my mother-in-law's house just a few weeks back. My sister-in-law was there with her new boyfriend, and when we walked in, he said hello to my daughter. My daughter just looked at him and walked off. My wife followed her and said, 'Don't be so rude; go and say hello.' So my daughter went back to him and said, 'Hello, I don't like you', and walked off again. My wife followed her once more and said, 'You can't say that, it's so rude! Go and say sorry!' So she turned around, walked back to him and said, 'I'm sorry I don't like you.'

That daughter has just started secondary school. She's doing very well. She's very bright but still not great socially. She doesn't know when to shut up and she often feels anxious. It's good at her school, though, as they have a special hub she can go to when she's not coping. She didn't get any support like that at primary school because she didn't have a diagnosis. That was my fault really because I didn't want her labelled. I understand now that a diagnosis can help. It can help to make sense of everything, and as a family, we've learnt how it can get you support. My eldest four kids have left home and aren't interested in getting diagnosed. To be honest, I don't see how it can help them now anyway. It's different with the younger ones, though. We want them to get as much support as they can. It's why my wife's visiting a special school today for our three-year-old. He's a bit of a nightmare, to be honest; there's no way he's going to cope in mainstream.

The four-year-old's not too bad but she still needs extra support. My wife and I had a meeting with her teacher the other day. The teacher commented on how our daughter had lots of friends. My wife pointed out that that wasn't true. She said, 'Lots of children talk to her, but if you ask her, she says she only has one friend, just one child that she chooses to speak to.' Later that week, our daughter was invited to a birthday party. She was adamant that the boy whose party it was wasn't her friend. She said, 'He doesn't talk to me, so I don't know why he's invited me to his party. He's not my friend, he talks to one other child and his Spiderman figures, but not me.' My wife said, 'Well, maybe he's autistic. Maybe he just doesn't know how to talk to you.' Our daughter said, 'Well, if he doesn't talk to me and I don't talk to him, how am I supposed to know that he's my friend?' I turned to my wife and said, 'Well, I'd like to know as well. How do you tell if someone's your friend?' My wife just looked at me and laughed, but I was being serious. The next day I asked a few people at the garage where I work, 'How do you know if someone's your friend?' They just looked very puzzled and couldn't give me an answer.

I get on all right with the people at work. I've been there 20 years. They haven't sacked me yet, so I must be good at what I do. I can't remember my own phone number, but I can take cars apart and put them back together. I've always enjoyed being around cars. I used to spend lots of time hiding in our garage as a child. It made sense to become a mechanic. The only thing I don't like is speaking to the public. Like my eldest daughter, I can get quite anxious in social situations. I worry about it a lot and have almost quit so many times because of it. Like tomorrow, I know I've got to speak to a customer and I didn't sleep at all last night worrying about it. I hope I can sleep tonight.

Lea

Empathizer

I believe that the idea of social conventions is obsolete. We are living in a time where diversity is celebrated more and more. This means celebrating *all* differences.

I've been out and proud as a lesbian for 27 years. I believe in a higher power, a collective consciousness; not some bearded man up above in the sky. I was raised in a liberal Presbyterian church and my family were very involved in participating in church activities. Our church was very accepting and loving. I've come to believe that the Bible was written as a sort of group of guidelines and cautionary tales during a time when people were basically running amok. I see many of the stories contained therein much like fables.

Growing up, I knew I was a bit different, but I didn't understand why. I did some strange things. I wet the bed until second grade. I identified mostly with adult women, of whom I had many that I counted as friends. I'd invite my peers over to play, then would tire of the social interaction after about half an hour, go into my room and shut the door. My older sister would have to play with them until it was time for them to go home. I liked to (and still prefer to) sleep naked due to my sensory issues. I was very introverted, so I didn't have much knowledge of what my peers were doing. When I went to my first slumber party at the age of eight (you can see where this is going…), it came time for bed and I stripped off all my clothes. It never occurred to me that the other girls would see that as strange, and I was teased mercilessly as a result. That is not a happy childhood memory.

My most significant coping mechanism was isolating myself. This carried over into adulthood. I was so much smarter than my peers that I think many of my differences were attributed to my above-average intellect and just being a 'quirky' kid. I'm sure it's why I flew under the radar until I recognized my autism and decided to get formally diagnosed. Over the years, I've developed so many intricate coping mechanisms in an effort to 'pass'. They are so ingrained in my way of being that although I know they're there, I can't tell you their specifics.

I was formally diagnosed at 43 with Asperger's, inattentive-type ADHD, social phobia, generalized anxiety disorder and dysthymia. That being said, I believe that all of the diagnoses aside from autism are just pieces of my autism that were separated out during the testing process. It all feels very intertwined to me.

I currently live in my own home by myself, with three cats, my beloved dog and a really cool sugar glider. Normally, the first thing I do in the morning is pick up my phone, hoping there are no necessary time-sensitive human interactions awaiting me. If I'm lucky and there aren't, I usually send my love a good-morning text. I then move on to games on my phone. If I'm successful in completing these challenges, I feel like I'll have a good day.

I complete my entire showering/grooming process in exactly the same way each morning. Same order, same procedure. If I skip a step, try to do things out of order, or something interrupts me, I get very flustered and am likely to forget what's next. After my shower I dress by putting my clothes on in the same order too. The entire process is scripted; sometimes I think it's the only thing that soothes me enough to get going each day. While I'm choosing my clothes, I pay special attention to the tasks ahead. If I know that I'll get to do things that are comfortable, then I wear very soft and comfortable clothing. If I know that my day will be stressful, then I'll choose to wear something less comfortable, as the feeling of more comfortable clothing will often distract me from the discomfort of what I am forced to do externally. I know that this sounds somewhat backward, and I know that it makes little sense. But it works for me. It's a coping mechanism, however strange.

Most of the thoughts that cause me stress in my day-to-day life depend on the tasks ahead of me. If I am forced to be social, then I worry constantly about whether I will do or say something that's deemed socially inappropriate, whether people will view me as not being smart. I was blessed with an IQ of 156, so this isn't a realistic issue, except for the fact that my misunderstanding of social expectations sometimes supersedes my intellect.

As weird as it may sound, I don't know that I ever feel 'happy'. The highest level of satisfaction for me comes in feeling content and soothed rather than happy. My special interests have always soothed me: animals, trees and shrubs, medicine, serial killers and true crime. My wife makes me feel soothed. As do babies and animals. My daughter (who is 26 years old) understands me on a very deep level, and that is soothing. She's a cook for a large organization that houses people with developmental disabilities/mental illnesses. So she understands the scope of the spectrum. She's *very* proud and protective of me. Sometimes too protective, but I know it's always born of love. She understands my needs and is very skilled at helping me navigate, should I get into a tricky situation. It's been my greatest achievement – raising a kind, compassionate, loving, brilliant, funny, thoughtful, empathetic young woman – hands down. She is all the best parts of me. She probably comes the closest to making me feel what people would consider 'happy', but in all honesty I feel the safest and most content when I am home alone with my dog. The fewer the demands, the better.

My background and education is in nursing, but once I started practicing, I realized I hated it. So I found a way to use my medical knowledge and education without being a practicing nurse. I started managing a group home for adults with developmental disabilities and mental illnesses. I worked well with people on the spectrum because I innately understood their needs. Over the years, I realized that I was like them in many ways. I didn't have an 'Aha!' moment, rather a slow realization of like-mindedness. When I was diagnosed, I was very open at work about having autism. Ironically, I don't think my superiors were too happy. I got the impression they felt like it would somehow make me seem less capable in others' eyes. Considering the emphasis in their mission statement on empowering people with differing abilities, I found this incredibly backward. It felt like they expected me to feel too ashamed to share my diagnosis. I'd been there seven years and I'd always been a superstar at work due to being so rule-oriented, but after my diagnosis people seemed to feel the need to tell me, 'Good job.' It felt like a pat on the head for the autistic girl. I didn't like it. It's the reason I left. The way that people treated me had changed and I found it terribly offensive.

Unless I tell them, I don't think that other people realize I have autism. Most of the behaviors that define it for me either occur internally or are just seen as a bit of social anxiety or awkwardness. When I do tell people, they often either treat me like I'm mentally retarded or argue with me in disbelief. I think it's because it's not readily apparent; they think if they can't see it, it doesn't exist.

I would like to be seen by the neurotypical population as a person with autism who is a survivor. I would like to be known for my compassion, insight and tenacity. I have no interest in hiding or blending in with the neurotypical population. I am not ashamed to have autism, and I think that the level at which I function puts me in the unique position of being able to educate neurotypical people about autism. I have done a lot of public speaking to this end, and I sit on the board of directors for my local autism society.

I don't really see the aspects of my autism as positive or negative, just different. I think there's value in looking at things through a perspective that is born from different wiring. It can be a very positive addition in many situations.

My father *totally* has autism. He also has very few coping mechanisms and a hurtful level of oblivion. Interestingly, my daughter has some behaviors that are autism-like. I think it's because she was raised solely by me; she's become a product of her environment. I'm pretty sure she's not actually on the spectrum.

I've had a series of complicated romantic relationships in

adulthood. I haven't always chosen healthy partners (alcoholics, narcissists, etc.). I've been legally married the once, and although we divorced, we are still very much together. Blending our families (she has three teenagers, two of whom have autism) proved to be too much for us to remain cohabitating. We love each other on the deepest of levels, though, and plan to remain together, remarry and co-habit once again when her children have grown up and moved out. It's very complicated. But she is also on the spectrum, so we understand each other better than anyone else in our lives ever has. Autism made the divorce infinitely harder because I was so depressed at the time. I really struggled to understand and navigate all the sadness, anger, resentment and loss that came with that experience. I was unable to articulate when I needed help or support from those around me. It was a terribly tragic and lonely time. But we know that we are one another's person, and we are comfortable with the way things are for the time being.

I've had frequent bouts of depression in the past, sometimes debilitating and very long-lasting. Sometimes it has caused my executive functioning to slow to a crawl. This has made the depression even worse because it's shone a spotlight on my disability and made me feel useless, hopeless and helpless. I think that my tendency to not look too far into the future and the fact that I don't really understand what it means to feel 'happy' are factors that can sometimes complicate my ability to pull myself out of depression.

I wish I could communicate more effectively in general. Especially during times of stress or high emotion. I've been known to inadvertently hurt people's feelings, and I *never* want to hurt anyone's feelings!

I am told that I am *waaaay* too direct and even that I am too truthful at times. Apparently, I can come across as rude, judgmental, cold and condescending. I deal with this most effectively by getting a feel for my audience, as I know that different people require different communication styles. I also do my best to soften my approach. I'm not always very successful with this, and it's caused a myriad of problems for me as a manager, a wife and also as a stepmother. It doesn't tend to cause any issues with my biological daughter, though, as she has known me to be the way that I am for her entire existence. She understands me and rarely, if ever, misreads my tone.

I've been in therapy numerous times, mostly to help me navigate periods of stress and anxiety. I've never specifically viewed this as a support for my autism, although I suppose that's been part of it. Depending on the therapist, I have found it totally useless, extremely helpful and everything in between. It's the only support I've ever required.

I'm glad to see more people with autism in the forefront on television shows and the like, but I think that they still have a long way to go in not portraying us all as easily identifiable, over the top, or as having unrealistic expectations and/or needs. I think we need to get more *real* information out into the world about autism. It needs to be provided by autistics themselves. Only then can we bring about more positive changes and universal understanding.

I'd like to develop a program that can be used with school-age kids to help them learn about autism, what it means to be autistic, how to have a relationship with a person on the spectrum, and how to help their peers with autism develop a sense of belonging and community. I believe that this exists for teachers, but not so much for students. Currently, these kids with autism are thrown into mainstream classes in the name of integration, but their peers aren't provided with the tools to build relationships with them. This immediately creates a sense of isolation for the child with autism. It's often followed by bullying and consequent trauma. Even though I 'passed' as neurotypical, I still felt these things. I had a lot of difficulty building relationships with people my own age and I'd like to be part of changing that.

Rhiannon
Idealist

Despite being born in Australia, my soul feels most at home in the language and culture of Wales; in a world of Celtic mythology. I've spent a lot of time over there, feel accepted over there. But I'll never be accepted over here. Not in this Anglo-society. I respect indigenous Australia, but this is not my land.

I was born into a family who didn't understand me. We moved around the world every few years and as a result I ended up going to 14 different schools. I felt isolated, irrelevant and unwanted. I tried to be good, to be liked, but I was inherently 'difficult by nature', or so I was told. For some strange reason, people had to be 'patient' with me. I didn't understand why. I was quiet and worked hard, extremely hard. But it was never quite hard enough.

Despite trying hard, I failed in everything. Everything except art. Teachers punished me when I asked them to repeat themselves, even though I genuinely didn't hear what they said. Later, I discovered that I had heard them; I just couldn't comprehend what they had said. It's called auditory processing disorder, but they didn't know much about APD or autism back then, especially high-functioning autism in girls. People just looked at me as if I was stupid.

Occasionally, I got into trouble, and when I did, it hurt – it really hurt! I felt everything too much. When I was bullied by other kids, told off by the teacher for things I didn't understand, or misinterpreted by my parents, I would hide if I could, and cry. My panic was worse if I couldn't escape, because showing emotion meant I'd be punished all over again. I learnt to keep my distance from people. My saving grace was my imagination. I created worlds in my head and lived there to escape this world. Daydreams became compulsive. They were more real than the reality everyone else lived in.

By the time I got to high school, my parents were told I wouldn't get past year 10. I felt terrified I'd be rejected by the school system and have nowhere to go. Even though I struggled with the work, it was my only stability and I needed it. Things got worse at home, so I tried forcing myself to be smart. I remember staring at myself in the mirror saying, 'You're smart, you're smart.' I forced myself through textbooks, despite having meltdowns where I'd punch myself, throw books against the wall. I couldn't have meltdowns around people, though. Around people I was mute.

By year 10 I got the award for the most improved student in the school, went on to year 11 in the middle stream. I pushed myself so hard that my perfectionism manifested itself in under-eating and over-exercising. By year 12, I got the grades to get into university. In the final year of uni, I got a distinction in honours, went on to become a psychologist.

My job now involves getting up early, very early, catching a train into the city. I'm enthusiastic because I know for two hours I can escape into my world of fantasy and imagination, i.e. I can get on with my writing. Once at work, I put on my mask, focus on making money so I can afford to get back to Wales.

My job now is good. So good in fact I sometimes feel guilty because I'm so deeply unhappy, skirting around depression and intense frustration. I get frustrated at not being able to speak Welsh out in the community without looking like a freak. I curse the English language regularly; I speak to myself in Welsh. Sometimes I get wafts of memories that take me back to Wales when I'm working and it's like I'm really back there. I wonder if there's a parallel reality where I'm actually there right now.

I struggle with not shrinking too far into my daydreams and detaching from the world for too long. Ironically, it's learning Welsh that demands I interact with people. It drives me to travel and to socialise.

It was only when I started to write fiction and learn Welsh that I really began to find and accept myself. Between these two passions I became interested in grammar, in both English and in Welsh. It's a work in progress, but I've had short stories published. I hope the same happens with a novel. And hopefully it'll be published in Welsh!

Gilbert

Scholar

Quite frankly, Asperger's is the least of my problems. I currently have bipolar type II disorder, generalized anxiety disorder, major depression, post-traumatic stress disorder, attention deficit disorder, obsessive compulsive disorder, seasonal affective disorder, undiagnosed fatigue, panic attacks, an attachment disorder, an eating disorder, celiac disease, irritable bowel syndrome, intermittent pain, intermittent gastritis, extreme hypertension, low testosterone, erectile dysfunction and Tourette's.

I'm currently too incapacitated to work. It wasn't always this way.

I used to wake at 7am and, assuming it was one of the alternating weeks in which I had my son, try to wake him up, shower and dress. In later years there'd be a bowl of marijuana thrown in there, before my second attempt to wake him up while also making his lunch. My third attempt would be successful. I'd then drive him to school and go on to my work.

Once there, I'd take care of various academic chores and teach some classes, skip lunch and prepare for the next ones.

I never felt the need to discuss my Asperger's unless a student specifically identified as an Aspie. Admitting to shared conditions tended to validate and empower my students. It improved my bond with them.

After lessons, I'd pick up my son and drive us home. I'd then typically either smoke another bowl or pass out due to fatigue while my son watched cartoons. Afterwards I'd make a simple dinner for him (often requiring him to wake me up from my fatigue-induced nap), eat whatever part he did not eat, have him take a shower. Usually by then it was time for his bed. I would put him down, then retreat to play computer games or pass out.

Looking back, I realize I was overwhelmed by the amount of work I had to do. I was convinced I was not doing enough (probably true), and chronically fatigued from years of being overstressed.

One of my biggest issues throughout my life has been my hypersexuality. As a teenager, I had a girlfriend who had a conveniently liberal grandmother. As a result, I was used to having sex at least once a day. My (now ex) wife lost interest in sex with me when our son was born. I subsequently spent a great deal of time suppressing my sex drive so as not to cause a problem in our somewhat emotionally abusive (her, not me) relationship. She informed me that my sex drive was apparently unusually high, a fact she said she hadn't realized when we first met. She demanded an open relationship even though that wasn't what I wanted.

After the divorce, I pursued monogamous and caring relationships based on sex. The internet helped me succeed. I conducted a systematic survey of some 14 dating sites (including pure-sex sites, excluding overly religious, conservative or niche sites) and found which ones worked best for me. I then learned to narrow choices down to likely candidates. I learned to establish rapport online before meeting. This put me at ease and allowed me to be flirtatious, confident and simply competent. Not to brag, but I almost always got second dates, and when I didn't, the feeling was mutual.

During this time, I also flitted about the local polyamorous, swinger and kink communities. I found I liked the latter best. I became a practicing sensual dominant – a role that worked well for me, as my timidity, inability to interact and emotional abuse had rendered me incapable of asking for what I needed in bed. Being in control alleviated the relevant burdens. I emphasized positive reinforcement over pain.

In turn this led to a life of BDSM (bondage, discipline/domination, sadism/submission and masochism) polygamy. I had two exclusive girlfriends, both of whom knew about the other. Time was shared between them, permitting me to have sex at least once a night when I didn't have my son.

The first major blow to this routine was the early onset, in my late 30s, of erectile dysfunction. Although treatable, it served a severe blow to my sense of self-worth. I used to take great pride in being able to perform well for long periods of time, but suddenly erectile dysfunction, coupled with extreme fatigue, left me, in my opinion, a consistent underperformer.

My reduction in self-worth led to a cascade of problems. Increasing feelings of vulnerability led to leaving one girlfriend and adding stress to my relationship with the other. I managed to control some of this with the help of marijuana, but then I began sleeping with former students. This caused a great deal of difficulty for my (remaining) girlfriend, who subsequently left me too.

My debts spiraled, and I was evicted from my doctoral program. I subsequently attempted to finish my dissertation (under another advisor) while working three jobs. Fatigue built up as I tried to keep up with a punishing exercise routine in martial arts to set a good example for my son. After seven years I had a breakdown and was hospitalized for expressing signs of acute hypomania.

One former student has stood by me throughout all of this. She took care of me, visited me in the hospital, invited me to live with her just as I was being removed from my previous dwelling. This young lady has an autistic daughter who was only diagnosed this year. She herself is also an Aspie. We've had quite a few things to overcome since getting together. She was hypothyroid, then her father died, then she was diagnosed with Sjogren's disease (one of the lupus-complex autoimmune disorders). Her sex drive has dropped to nil, and I have not had sex in almost four months. We've not had mutually enjoyable, connected sex in about a year.

I love her but I'm sexless without a job (I lost it during my breakdown). I have no income (trying to get disability) and no marijuana (too expensive). I live in a house we can't afford (her father owned it), together with an autistic child. I can only see my son on weekends because his mother moved to a better school district, and I moved too far away (the terms of the divorce limited where we could live). I can't eat gluten because of my celiac disease and I'm also partially lactose-intolerant. My one satisfaction is that none of my problems appear to have been passed on down to my son.

Colin

Techie

It's at times like Christmas that I realise how lonely I am at work. Last year there was a special festive buffet lunch we all had to go to. I sat in the vicinity of colleagues from the same pod of desks as me, but I was soon shunted along so a more popular member of staff from the other side of the office could get in. There were about 80 of us altogether. Everyone else was in full conversation with the people around them – and then there was me. It was as if I didn't exist, I didn't count. Not a word was spoken to me. It was uncomfortable, stressful and very upsetting. I tried to hold out as long as the anxiety would let me, a total of about 20 minutes. Then I had to get out.

Christmas is always a hard time for me on many levels. As a kid, I used to find where the presents were hidden, carefully open them, then re-wrap them so I knew what I was getting. I still hate surprises to this day.

The worst part for me as an adult is that I go into a panic attack just at the thought of buying gifts. The crowds are also just that bit more unnerving at Christmas time. I therefore avoid shops from November through till February. As a result,

I've never been able to get my wife a proper Christmas present. Even if I make it to the shops, I just go into 'Aspie shutdown'. I completely cease to function beyond breathing and escaping. My wife used to think I was mean when I didn't get her anything, but now she understands how hard I find it. I'll buy her anything she wants but I can't attach a label like Christmas onto it. Birthday presents have exactly the same effect on me. Paralysing fear and anxiety. And it destroys me every year that I can't, even though she told me years ago not to bother anyway...

My reality can be a fragile place to live in. Sometimes I can go from being OK and being able to hold a normal conversation to planning my own suicide in detail in less than 90 seconds flat. All it takes is a simple, misconstrued word.

I guess I see the world through a sort of hamster ball. I can explore, I can see the world around me, but it's a place I can only observe and not interact with. When I'm feeling fragile, edgy, nervous, the hamster ball seems to shrink and gets tighter around me, to the point where it freezes me in place, unable to move, hardly able to breathe. I have a small stock of diazepam in my wallet all the time, and it's at times like this that it helps me to cope.

I also have trouble associating with intimacy. I might have the bits, but they don't belong to me; it feels awkward to be in any sort of intimate situation – distressing even. I've never been able to relax and enjoy the pleasures of the 'here and now', even though, to a large extent, I only live in the here and now. Intimacy is like someone has stuck a dildo to the outside of the hamster ball – it's not mine, I can't use it. I still have a yearning to be close to someone, but I'm locked inside this prison.

I was brought up in a broken home; my parents divorced

when I was five. My mother decided she was going to have an affair, and eventually married the other man. I remember there being a sort of menace about him that never felt right. I found out years later that he had children with a previous wife, and there must have been some sort of court order barring him from contact as my mother knew nothing about their existence. My dad wanted to keep me, and I remember sitting in his car outside the court, hearing him say, 'Sorry, son, you've got to go with her.'

In retrospect, I realise there was a good chance my mother was autistic too. Unfortunately, the damage was done as a child to make sure any feelings for her quickly vanished. She squirted dish soap in my mouth when she thought I said something rude or had sworn. She even held a knife to my throat. One day, after years of threats to put me in a children's home, she took me on a visit to a 'home for maladjusted children'. It was a secure unit that had held several high-profile adolescent murderers. I didn't want anything to do with her after that.

I guess it's not surprising I was writing suicide notes from quite a young age. I've always mentally gone down the self-harm route when stressed. I probably wouldn't have made it to my teenage years if it wasn't for my dad. I remember him driving me back to my mother's after being with him for a weekend. Only this time he didn't leave me there. The words 'He's coming home with me' came as a shock to us all.

I was diagnosed with Asperger's at 40 after seeing an article on the news. It took me three years to get it made official. This was due to so many conversations with doctors that went along the lines of 'If I had a pound for every time someone came in and said they had something because they saw it on TV...'

I quickly realised there was nothing around here for adults with autism, so I helped create a hub in an office in a nearby town. It's where people with autism can come and meet each other. A space to share life with like-minded people. Together we put in a request for a grant to buy equipment. We ended up getting twice what we asked for. So we've now got a wide range of stuff from Lego to a telescope to help people follow their own interests.

Even though I look functional, my executive functioning is quite badly broken. I used to wear the same clothes, including underwear, for a week or more. I can go weeks, even months, without remembering to brush my teeth.

Since 1995 I've had back problems where I can't stand for more than a few minutes, but although I'm in pain, I can't describe where the pain is. The autism part of me means that it takes a huge amount of effort to try to get issues looked at. If I get ignored or given the brush-off, I literally can't bring it up again. It took me 15 years to try to get my pain looked at after my first attempt. That's 15 years in too much pain to walk, shop or make love to my wife. I was eventually told it was chronic pain syndrome, where the brain continues to get flooded by pain reports from the nervous system, even if the problem isn't there anymore.

I'm now on seven different drugs to try to manage the pain. They're barely working, but if I up them, they leave me too sedated to drive or work safely.

My wife reckons getting a new dog has given me a new lease of life, effectively saved me. Before we got her, I'd been under a lot of stress at work. My wages had been cut and my back pain was severe. My anxiety was constant. I was a jittery, shaky mess.

I remember realising back then that the last time the panic had subsided was two years ago in August. For a grand total of 15 minutes. It had been so out of the ordinary for me I even mentioned it to my wife: 'I feel OK today!' Anyway, like I said, my anxiety was constant. And then, just a while after our old dog had passed away, I saw a Labrador on one of the dog rescue sites we follow. We passed all the vetting procedures with a single call to our vet. We should have known it was all a bit too easy, that she'd be a bit of a handful. The advert said: 'Experienced owner required.' She was a complete nightmare: seven months old, with zero training. Running around after the crazy mutt was enough to stop me dwelling on my issues quite so much. Five years on, she's a little sweetheart – a great unofficial therapy dog.

Vometia

Bass Player

I'm a trans-lesbian autistic sysadmin Christian bass player who likes video games, shoes, beer and swords. Sadly, Northumbrian is not a nationality, so I'll have to say I'm British of largely Scottish descent with some American and Irish thrown in for good measure.

When I was younger, we lived in a very child-friendly area – lots of safe, open, green spaces, lots of children my own age milling about. My parents were pretty tough on me. They 'treated' my ADHD and ASD with shaming, humiliation, threats, shouting and occasional violence. They now claim that autism was unknown when I was growing up. This clearly wasn't true as I was often threatened with being sent to 'the special school' if I didn't behave. They never attempted to have me properly assessed. That time had a profound and negative impact on me and probably plays a large part in my current agoraphobia and my general inability to cope. The diagnosis has gone a small way to heal that damage.

It was a random online acquaintance who said something innocuous about her autistic brother being a gamer that made all the assumptions unravel. I realised I could be both autistic and still my own person.

My days are fairly routine. I have assorted random sleep problems and spend most nights waking up repeatedly. At some point I'll become so fatigued with trying to sleep that I'll give up and get up for the day. I take my morning cocktail of medications, gulping them down with water from my freebie Guinness glass. It has a small lid so that the visiting cat doesn't help herself. Nothing worse than drinking from a glass only to see suspicious hairs floating on top. I check out the usual stuff online, look at the daily comic strips, ban new spammers from the forums I manage. When I'm not too exhausted to engage with her, I go and play with the cat. I then annoy my girlfriend until she gets up.

Next is the worst part of the day: exercise. Forty minutes of wandering up and down the stairs is never inspiring. I spend the time listening to music, usually Electric Six, best known for the frankly ludicrous 'Gay Bar'. Their upbeat silliness is generally a fair guarantee that the unpleasantness will be completed together with the minimum amount of trauma. Afterwards I'll run the bath, checking it over for stray hairs beforehand. I then partly dress. Hopefully, I'll remember the deodorant (this week's is apparently cucumber-scented; it smells vaguely of Pimm's to me), then I'll smear hormones all over my legs and settle down in front of the computer.

The rest of the day passes in much the same way: settled in front of the computer, progressively becoming more and more dressed.

Midday approaches and anxiety rises. It's in line with the postie approaching. Will he have anything for me? Will it be nice, or will it be from the bank, insurer or hospital?

Beer is sort of lunch. Come late afternoon, though, I'm thinking about real food. I want a curry because I always want a curry. I do the cooking, but it can be difficult. I'm not allowed to play with knives; I'm too clumsy and irresponsible. I still do it, though, because my girlfriend does all the other stuff – the gnarly business like dealing with people and the vacuum cleaner. We call him Bastard. She views him with affection, but I consider him to be a menace. He's over 20 years old now and as cantankerous as the day he was made.

After dinner, worrying thoughts try to elbow their way in, so that's when I start the video games; shooting mutants always takes my mind off things. Only problem is, I start to feel progressively more awake the more distant I become from the excruciation that was last night's sleep. I no longer want to go to bed. Eventually, I relent. Evening medications again: just statins. It used to include sleeping pills, but they have a habit of making me depressed. Since I no longer take sleeping pills, I lie awake for the next hour or so, becoming more and more bored and frustrated. I eventually get up again until I'm ready for a second try. The rest of the night continues in much the same vein.

I find happiness to be an elusive thing. To me it involves accomplishing something, gaining some degree of recognition – preferably the former leading eventually to the latter. Recognition seems to be important to me, partly because perhaps I didn't get enough of it earlier in life, and partly because my social interaction is so very limited nowadays; that, combined with my ASD, means I need quite a clear message that I've somehow managed to make a difference somewhere.

The negatives of my ASD are the same as the positives. What

some people might call an obsession, I would call attention to detail, problem solving, determination to see something through. Unfortunately, the determination can be extremely persistent and ultimately exhausting. It's practically impossible for me to switch off.

I try to remain optimistic about my future. I've succeeded in making some positive differences to my life and other people's, and this makes me feel good. It's unfortunate, though, that society isn't very ASD-friendly; ordinary people day to day are all right, but not enough organisations make any sort of provision for ASD people. This includes those that should know better. The autism doctors seemed quite resigned to this and stated that although the mental health services could offer specific help, they'd probably decline to do so. Which they did. 'Just call us,' they'd say. 'I can't,' I'd say. 'I have ASD and find it hard to use the phone.' 'Oh well, in that case I don't think there's anything else we can do to help you!'

All social situations are challenging for me. They cause severe anxiety beforehand. I usually cancel nearly all of them, and as a result I rarely see people outside of mandatory situations such as hospital appointments. I don't socialise, I never go down the pub and I don't take myself off on holiday. There was, however, a restaurant in town which I used to view as a 'safe space'. I'd go there every few weeks on a quiet afternoon, but unfortunately it closed down. Social media is therefore a life-saver. It's immensely useful to people like me who would otherwise be extremely isolated.

Ordinary people mostly don't care about my autism. They see an individual first rather than some umbrella term. Employers, agencies and the media are a different story. In my experience, we tend to be seen as a problem, a curiosity, something to be exploited.

I used to work with computers. Even though I found the commuting to be highly stressful – agoraphobia, stress and information overload left me shattered before I'd even started – I did it. I'd spend the day in a distracting office with rude, shoulder-surfing managers talking about me rather than to me. I was expected to do unpaid overtime where I had nothing to do; I was expected to be on constant unpaid on-call duties. I spent my days filling in timesheets, phoning people, doing stupid and mostly pointless admin tasks instead of my job. I felt that my ASD helped me with my actual job: the hyper-focus and obsessive problem-solving tended to be assets, even if the ability to disconnect from the task in hand could often feel frustrating. Unfortunately, though, it made the non-job elements much more distracting and distressing. Which was a shame. I enjoyed what my job actually entailed (sysadmin and programming). I just didn't enjoy the non-productive elements that went with it. Workplaces are not very ASD-friendly. And they only seem to be getting worse. After years of forcing myself to put up with it, it all became too much. I haven't worked now for years.

I think a lot of it comes down to the management. A good manager protects their staff from the pointless politics and other nonsense, whereas a bad manager tends to amplify them, sometimes significantly. At one point when I was working, my manager resigned. They weren't replaced for a whole year. It was the most productive working environment, with the highest morale, that I've ever had the luck to experience.

If ASD is a disorder, it could be argued that it's a disorder of society for having too narrow a view of what comprises an acceptable human being. We're constantly told that a person's entire worth is based on whether they're in a job, preferably high-paying, and nothing to do with whether or not they're a decent human being or if they actually contribute anything positive to society. The pointlessness and lack of accessibility of the workplace seem to make work a pointlessly difficult endeavour altogether.

Although I feel anger about how autistic people are treated, I also feel the same amount of optimism. I think things will change. When a society becomes this unenlightened, I think Yazz is right: 'The Only Way is Up.' It's just taking its own sweet time.

Murphy

Kidult

People accept that I'm different. Sometimes, though, I blame how I am on my autism, when I know deep down I'm just being a twat.

I work at home one day a week. I love it because I can be so productive. The rest of the time, it's an effort to get up, an effort that gets progressively more difficult as the week progresses. I live alone with my two cats in a flat just a ten-minute walk from my job at the local council.

My desk at work is always full of crap. It includes my magic 'just in case' bag of medication. I take a lot of painkillers and so on for chronic pain-management conditions including arthritis. I find sitting all day can be very painful, but I don't like taking breaks; I like to get on with things instead.

My job involves lots of sequential activities, so lots of concentration is required.

Unfortunately, I'm not very good at concentrating. I constantly get bombarded by emails from people asking me to do stuff for them such as booking rooms and making people's time available. I get overwhelmed by following all the steps and I struggle to multi-task; I need to fulfil whatever I'm doing before moving on. I can feel when I'm getting frustrated. I start picking up environmental sounds around me. The noise cuts through everything else and I get angry. Angry at myself and angry at everyone else because it doesn't bother them. I use my ear defenders, but that's only OK if no one needs to talk to me. If it all gets too much, I take time out.

I have banter with people at work; it's a pleasant, humorous environment and the people are pleasant enough. My employers are aware of my autism, but, like me, they don't fully understand it yet – the impact it can have. I used to think they saw me only as a twat, but I think their views have changed as I've become better at controlling my grumpiness. Having had clinical assessments and a report has helped because they are more forgiving, more supportive of ways to adapt for my needs. I can't fault them as individuals or as an organisation for how flexible they've been to me.

On work days, at about half two I start getting uncomfortable and struggling to cope. I get tired and want to go home, lock myself away from the world again. Not snapping at people becomes more of a challenge.

There's often the sound of a kid shouting from somewhere within our open-plan office. I assume he has learning disabilities, that he's randomly crying out in distress. I struggle to empathise with him, which I feel guilty about, but in the moment he just annoys me.

I finally leave at half four. Once home, I spend the evening in front of the telly. My viewing's interspersed with interacting with people on Facebook. I put everything on there, no matter how banal or impressive – when I feed my cats, the consistency of my farts. My life is social media. I can be more 'me' on there; I can be a part of the wider world.

Sometimes I still have the energy to cook for myself; other times I just eat crap. I go to bed about 7pm, watch TV until I fall asleep about midnight.

I like to be in control of everything that I do, and it freaks me out if things occur on someone else's terms.

I've always worried about why other people have girlfriends and families and social lives, but I don't. I live in a world of isolation, sometimes by choice to avoid environmental overload such as crowds and noises, and sometimes because of my inability to manage the relationship cues.

I've always been aware that I struggle with relationship boundaries, but I haven't been aware enough to stop it being a problem. I attend counselling and have done for a while due to frequent depression and suicidal thoughts surrounding my differences. I've tried to kill myself three times, roughly once a decade during my adult life. Counselling has helped me see the ways in which just being me is OK. I still struggle, though, with the fact that my differences can be so isolating.

Thinking about it, I don't think there's enough support out there for newly diagnosed adults. By this I mean those who are self-diagnosed as well as those with an official diagnosis. You find out it's autism and then you're alone. I'm lucky to have support from the counselling service that my friend runs. She knows quite a lot about mental health and neurodiversity. If it wasn't for her, I'd be much more in the dark.

As well as attending counselling, I've also completed a counselling degree. The knowledge I gained from my studies prompted me to see a psychologist. I was given a diagnosis, just a month or two ago, of executive functioning disorder. They told me that if I'd been tested as a child, I would have been diagnosed with autism and ADHD. Because of this, I don't think I'm just being grumpy and anti-social anymore. It makes sense. In confrontations I've tended to think it was the other person with the problems. Now I realise it might have been me that said something rude or hurtful and not realised. Now I can see that I just don't get some of the social cues. I don't always pick up on nuance and social etiquette; I can be a blunt instrument of communication. Being able to reflect upon this, I'm more open now to listening when people make me aware I've crossed a line. I also judge myself less as I know there's a reason for it. It's not because I'm an idiot or childish or thick or stupid or less. It's because I'm autistic.

Because of my autism, I feel like I missed out on a lot of what I see as a normal upbringing. I can see the distress my autism caused me, and I can see how poorly this distress was managed. People acted as though I was less capable. Sometimes they tried to make decisions for me, to 'care for me' by taking away my choices. As a result, I had less autonomy. As a result, I now live very self-sufficiently. I look after myself. I go away on childhood trips. I have adventures at the seaside. I'm happiest there – fish and chips and ice cream. Just me in the sun, enjoying the childhood I know I never had.

From a social point of view, I've got to the stage where I just want people to like me. Although I still expect rejection when I'm depressed, I'm gradually learning that people will accept me as I am. If I feel like crap, there are a few people I can reach out to who'll keep me busy with photography or similar activities, although I wouldn't reach out without prompting. I've spent too many years being unsure of where the boundaries are to confidently test them like that.

Ultimately, life hasn't turned out to be a bed of roses with 2.4 children and white picket fences. I'm too big. I'd like to lose weight. I'd like to get rid of my debts. I'd like to have the confidence to socialise without worrying about sensory interference or hurting other people's feelings. I haven't had romance and I'd have liked to have had children. Having said all of this, I like my life. I have two fur babies (my cats), I have my camera and my computer, my telly and my bed. I'm in control of what I do and I'm content.

Our 50s

Maria

Nurse

I was in management for about ten years but returned to a nursing role when I lost the drive for leadership. I'm currently working extra evening shifts to pay off my debts. It keeps me busy and there's lots of interaction with people. I work second shift, so I leave my apartment at lunchtime. My commute takes almost an hour, so I listen to library books on my phone. I work for eight hours, five days a week, and I'm also frequently on call.

I like to get everything at work done as quickly as possible, as efficiently as possible. I like everything to be very organized. In fact, I once quit a job because the nurse's station was such a dump! While I'm working, I'm hoping we get all surgeries done on time so that only a few of us need to remain to clean things up and prepare for the next day.

I'm not the troublemaker at work that I used to be. I'm enjoying my current job and have been here for a little over a year. I love working in the operating room because order and cleanliness is a must, and I have one patient at a time, who is always asleep.

I've done so much work on myself in 12-step programs over

the years, I'm no longer afraid of surgeons or people in general. Maintaining this control over my life, both at work and at home, is very important to me. I'm 13 years sober, 96 pounds lighter. I eat a very controlled vegan diet and I no longer smoke.

My environment at home is incredibly neat and clean too. You'd never know that I have three cats, two dogs, fish, rats and a snake. I need lots of time to think and do things in an orderly manner; being single allows me that. I love watching TV, movies and the news, although I'm usually doing something on my phone at the same time. I love crossword puzzles and I have no problem recalling medical facts I've learned over the years.

As a child, I loved science and cataloging things like insects. I was in a gifted program, but my family weren't supportive; I quit when math got too difficult. I'm awful at math! I love words so much, though. I have a knack for reading extremely quickly. I can write very well but I don't. Because I don't like the physical writing part!

I started drinking as a young teenager to fit in, had sex early on for the same reason. I never found anyone on my mental level, though. There were intelligent people, of course, but not deep. I got pregnant at 18 and got married.

I have a wonderful relationship with my teenage daughter. She's my best friend. There's one other person who I consider a close friend, but we rarely talk. She knows me and accepts me. I don't think I'm as devoted to her as she is to me. She fawns and gushes over me and I hate that. I don't really have any other friends. I like it that way.

I think the world sees me as being somewhat of a rebel. I have tattoos and piercings, I don't dress to impress, and I don't date or flirt.

I see neurotypicals as being oblivious to who I am. Nobody wants to get to know me. I feel that they are self-centered in this way, but they probably can't help it. I judge myself, monitor myself. When I feel I'm monopolizing things, I tone it down or back off. I want to do the right thing.

I'm a very logical person. If I could, I would get rid of stupid people who do not use facts to make decisions. After all, if something isn't logical, why do it? I'm currently trying to teach myself how to monitor my thoughts and actions to become a better person. I also want to make sure, though, that I remain true to myself.

Together with my sobriety, I've also taken up atheism. Because a god makes no sense to me. I don't blame my parents anymore for the mistakes that they made in the past. I rarely get angry. I've taught myself gratitude and I now know that my problems are nothing. I intend to get as much out of each day as I can. My life isn't exciting and I'm not close to any extended family anymore, but I'm happy. I'm a happy person every day.

It's difficult to peel away the layers of enabling and doing for others. I've been taken advantage of by my three adult children and now none of them are speaking to me. I've felt a lot of guilt over the years. It isn't easy, but I'm accepting of it.

As I've gotten older, I've become better at understanding things. I'm knowing myself, what I like and don't like. I wish my father were still alive, so I could talk to him about it. I think he had Asperger's. He's been deceased now for many years. Everyone thought of him as brilliant but eccentric. I think I'm very much like him. He was so smart, curmudgeonly and weird. He was a best friend and we talked about everything. He could never maintain a relationship, was always forlorn over being alone.

I've learned that relationships don't work for me either. I've been married and divorced now four times. I'd still like to meet someone, though – someone who is as interested in me as I am in them. Unfortunately, I've always ended up with people who come on strong at first, but then use me for my home or money. I seem to be attracted to addicts and alcoholics, party animals and those who are less intelligent than me. Since the menopause as well, I have no libido. That, coupled with antidepressants for anxiety, leaves me with no desire, thank heavens. I'm very insecure about my body; being naked with someone scares me. I know intellectually, though, that someone who really cared about me wouldn't mind. I've spent most of my life seeking love, but I'm yet to meet someone like that. I never thought I could live alone and be happy, but I do and I am. It's been five years now.

Corum

Artist

I very, very rarely discuss my feelings as I'm never really sure what they are. Although I understand things reasonably well on an intellectual level, I'm pretty useless when it comes to emotional matters. Emotionally, I'm just out of first grade.

My home is a sixth-floor flat/apartment in a 16-storey building. The building houses approximately 100 flats/apartments. It was built during the 1960s in response to the housing needs of the country. The 1960s saw a lot of social housing built here, not all of it to a particularly good standard. A failed experiment in social housing in my opinion. These tower blocks were supposed to create communities in the sky, but they seem to have led to alienation and a lack of personal responsibility. I'd guess that most of my contemporaries own their own homes. But it's not something that occurred to me earlier in my life; I saw home ownership as a long-term debt.

My flat is comfortable. It has two bedrooms. I use the smaller of the bedrooms as a studio of sorts; it's where I create my art. Ideally, I'd like some outdoor space, more distance between myself and the neighbours. The neighbourhood is OK, though.

It used to be a mining area, a rough-and-ready working-class area, but it's slowly changing. It's very multicultural but I don't see much interaction between the various ethnic or religious groups. I have no doubt it happens, but to a limited extent. I guess the old saying 'Birds of a feather stick together' holds true.

My days are fairly routine. After increasingly vivid dreams (the result of antidepressants), I make the first of innumerable mugs of coffee. I put on the news, smoke my first cigarette of the day, check the football gossip columns and my social media.

I've always had a distrust of authority and mainstream media, but current affairs still interest me. I like to keep abreast of what's happening in the world. I guess my views are liberal as I don't believe that anyone should arbitrarily hold authority over me. It's probably why I'm a republican and why, as a late teen, I held a belief in anarchist principles.

Around mid-morning I tend to nip out for small items such as milk or sugar, maybe tobacco. Once home, I lock the front door and change into shorts. I then start reading, watching YouTube or painting. I studied fine art as a mature student back before tuition fees came in. I studied printmaking and photo-media, used computers to manipulate images, then turned them into photo silk screens or etchings. The subjects I was dealing with in my art were social/political, though I was never really unequivocal. I preferred to use my images as a way of raising questions within the viewer. It's not my place to say if or how successful I was in that.

I'll carry on with whatever I'm doing till early evening, when I'll take a break for food. The evening will be spent doing the same again or playing the guitar badly.

Some may see my life as a lonely experience, but I don't.

I enjoy its simplicity and not having to deal with other people too much. I spend the vast majority of my time alone and I enjoy it that way. Keeping myself away from other people keeps me on track.

The only long-term relationship I've ever managed to maintain collapsed at the beginning of my studies. I wasn't attentive or very open emotionally. I was also using drugs as a way of coping with being in close proximity to others. This led to me being estranged from my baby daughter – something I found very difficult. My father then suffered a series of devastating strokes. He never fully recovered and passed away during my second year of studies.

Around this time I created a series of works based on missing people. I drank a lot, used non-prescription drugs. Inevitably, the pressure got too much, and I ended up on an ICU (intensive care unit). I'd taken an overdose of prescription drugs which were, ironically, prescribed to help me cope. I'm lucky (very lucky) to have survived, but I did. I managed to get through my final year, missing out on a first by only a few points. Most people would have seen it as a success, but at the time I felt like a failure. I'm proud of it now, though. That being said, I've done nothing to build on it. I've just floated through life, aimlessly drifting.

I moved to this city to be close to my daughter. She was diagnosed with Asperger's at a young age, classified as a special needs child at her school. I was diagnosed just last year. My daughter is now 24. We don't see each other very often or for very long. But I love her, and I think she loves me in her own way.

I have no thoughts on my personal future. I know at some

point it will all end. I try to make myself comfortable till that time arrives. I don't see much changing, barring a lottery win. For some time, it was a source of frustration, but I'm resigned to it now.

My day-to-day thoughts tend to revolve around abstract things such as where society is going or how much it has changed. I don't often share those thoughts. Words are difficult and often open to interpretation. I find it difficult to express my thoughts clearly enough for myself, so it's unlikely anyone else would find them easy to follow. I guess I'm quite guarded. I find it difficult to trust others. Too often I've misunderstood or been misunderstood. People have a tendency to lock people down. Once you express an opinion or thought, they find it difficult if you then change your mind.

I find a lot of human behaviour mystifying. I tend to see things in black and white, and find it very difficult to accept less in others. I also can't understand why people cannot or do not see things the way I do. I have difficulty in accepting dogmatic beliefs and have often taken contrary stances to try to shake another's dogmatic acceptance of ideas. I've always questioned things and as a child always supported the underdog. Maybe it's because I have no firmly held beliefs of my own and am comfortable changing my thinking and ideas with new data input.

Although I used to, I now no longer believe in 'isms'. They're ultimately divisive. I've tried to explain this to my daughter, using feminism as an example. I believe in equality of opportunity but not of outcome. And I can't understand the logic of saying, 'I'm a feminist and I believe in equality', when the very word 'feminism' cuts out half the world. I understand the arguments and fully agree that all females should be treated as equals of males. But I also believe we're a dimorphic species and we should celebrate our differences.

I guess I feel that political correctness is now being used to control people. It's not ultimately empowering – quite the opposite. We're living in a divided society. Current thoughts and trends are creating ever smaller subsets within humanity. I find it amazing that students would oppose free speech. Or require safe spaces. The gains we made in the 1960s are slowly being eroded away; we're losing our freedom. The worst thing is, we're happily giving it away.

Helen

Reader

I got pregnant the first time I had sex. I was 14. My older sister had already had a baby young. A well-meaning friend of the family decided I should go see a psychiatrist to help me decide what to do. I told the psychiatrist that I wanted to have the child. A week or so later, I found myself in hospital being injected in the womb with a drug to induce labour. I was told I was having a termination. I didn't realise how painful it would be and how long it would take. I was put in a room on my own as I made too much noise and I wasn't allowed any visitors. I was scared and in agony for two days. They gave me morphine to ease the pain. I soon learnt that that kind of drug could numb the world for me.

It's the hardest thing I've ever been through. It wiped out any trust I'd had in medical authority and paved the way for a 20-year addiction to opioid drugs. Because of this, I've never talked about my thoughts or life experiences to any medical professionals.

I left home at 16 and proceeded to have many sexual partners. I chose gentle men who were happy with the casual but friendly connection I wanted. I've always enjoyed sex. I've always thought of it as an important force for happiness. I've had a few long-term relationships, each of which ended mutually with no unpleasantness. I've had more lovers than friends. Sex is easy to understand; the murky world of friendships (especially with women) is fraught with misunderstandings.

I worked in the sex industry for about 20 years, eventually specialising in fantasy work. It suited me well as I was already acting around other people anyway. The apparently bizarre sexual fantasies therefore seemed no stranger to me than the general behaviour of most people. The sex act itself was easy to do with strangers as I have no religious/emotional connotations to using this part of my body for work. I can easily detach from myself. I did try a few other jobs, but I found dealing with the mainstream interests boring. I preferred the sex industry; it paid well, and I got to choose my own hours.

Now, though, I just have sex with my lover. It's totally different from the paid work. Sex now provides me with pleasure and an energy earthing; it helps to keep my stress levels down.

Before I met my lover, I was married for 13 years to a man 17 years younger than me. He suffered from severe anxiety episodes and frequently talked about suicide. He eventually made the decision to leave his body. I missed him a lot and I still wish that he could have found help for his problems. I respected his choice, though, to leave; his life, his death. I don't share the anger that some people do when they've lost a partner to suicide.

I currently identify as bisexual although all my long-term partners have been male. When I was younger, love was intense and poetic, fated and cosmic. Now with my lover of ten years, it is like a comfortable pair of pyjamas. There's total trust. We've both had previous relationships and we've both lost loved ones.

My lover is retired, and I've just been cured of a 30-year illness, hepatitis C. I don't need to work anymore, and my days are quite routine. I like it this way. When I first wake up, though, I often feel a deep sadness. My youngest sister died just over a year ago and a good friend about a month ago, both from the end effects of hepatitis C. I feel so lucky that I'm cured but sad that they are not. The sadness goes once I sit up in bed and read with the cat; its presence is gently soothing.

Our chicken run is close to the bedroom, and as I read, I listen to the rooster crowing and the chickens clucking. Their noise eventually gets me out of bed to feed them. I also feed Sally the dog and then the cats – Jimmy, who was a rescue case, and Roger the Lodger, a stray who turned up a few months ago. After the cats, I put some grain, peas and apples out next to a big bowl of water for the wild birds who live in the paddock next to us. They're getting tame and spend a lot of time here, sleeping up in the bamboo at night. There are also some Weka (flightless birds about the size of a chicken). They like a bit of dogfood.

After sorting out the animals, I soak some oats for porridge and make some tea and coffee. I then go back to bed where my lover will still be sleeping. I sit in bed and read, write or do puzzles. When my lover wakes up, we talk and usually make love. I do not like anyone but him touching me. I do not initiate hugs. I prefer to be touched firmly (which relaxes me) rather than lightly (which feels like distorted electricity). I then have a wash and do some yoga while he goes to the shop for the paper. We have breakfast at midday, watch the news on TV. I find the ads on the TV overwhelming and distracting, and after some time of negotiation with my lover, we now mute them (I've worn out mute buttons on remotes because of this). We then read the paper, check social media, emails and the weather forecast. I give the chickens any scraps from last night's dinner, collect their eggs and ruffle up the straw in their house. I then take the dog for a walk.

This is the first time in my life I've not worried about my future. I have a home for the rest of my days. I love hearing the rain on the roof as I lie in the arms of my lover. I'm not so keen on the hum of appliances on standby, but I love hearing the dog snoring on her bed and the rumble of the wood stove. I love seeing the mist coming up from the hills. Here I'm able to enjoy having a clear mind, not visiting others and not going out. My living situation suits me well and I enjoy the peace and quiet.

We've only been here for five years now. When we bought the house, it hadn't been lived in for some time. You couldn't open the back door for the overgrowth, and both the water tank and wood stove had rusted away. We didn't have any power for some time. Now that we've got indoor plumbing and electricity, it feels like we're living in luxury. There is even a solar-powered pump to get water up to the header tank, and solar-powered lights as well.

We have lots of bad weather here and power cuts, so it's good to have the back-up. My lover is an excellent gardener, so we're able to live for most of the year off our own produce too.

I believe that many of the residents of our little village here have Asperger's. It's a very isolated place so it tends to attract those who like a mountain range between themselves and the rest of humanity. The majority live alone. They're an interesting, eccentric lot. Everyone waves but most are too busy to visit. This means I have a lovely unsociable time. I have an internet connection, books I've not yet read and enough fabric to make comfortable clothes to last the rest of my days.

I'm very content but I still wish I was more graceful, that I could walk more lightly on this planet. I wish that I didn't constantly drop things in the kitchen or bang into things around the house. I can get very angry with myself for my clumsiness. The feeling passes more quickly nowadays, though, as I'm trying to be kinder to myself. Social media has helped me with this. I now know that I'm not the clumsiest person in the world. Knowing this heartens me. Social media has enabled me to contact people who speak my language. The idea that we can have this connection across the planet, without having to invade each other's space, is amazing.

I've only recently found out that I have Asperger's. I've just been bumbling about through life. I've got on OK, but now that I know about it, I feel capable of dealing with whatever comes my way. The strange thing about getting better from a long illness at my age is that when most people are beginning to feel worse than they did before, I'm beginning to feel better. I now have lots of energy for thinking. One of the effects of the long-term illness was brain fog, and it was not until it cleared, and my health returned, that I could see how my mind truly works. I know now that I'll never pass as neurotypical for long. This knowledge provides me with the freedom to give up the game of pretence and let my mind go free. The good thing about becoming an old woman is that no one cares what you do anyway. Back in my youth, I censored myself to fit in. In doing so, I ignored a big chunk of my intelligence and imagination. The brakes are off now, and I shall use every bit of my wondrous mind.

My lover is my only close friend. I do not wish to find any new friends unless an unexpected kindred soul comes my way. As a friendless child, I learnt to be self-sufficient and now I am comfortable with just my own company. I've been lucky, though. I've had a handful of friends in my life who were special, but they're gone now, and I don't think they are replaceable.

I'm unsure how the rest of the world sees me. I've given up trying to communicate with others, except on a shallow basis. I see neurotypicals as a different species that is intriguing to study. I am wary. The relatively new knowledge about Asperger's explains so much about my failed connections with others.

I was a quiet child. My mother says I did not cry much as a baby, and when she went to check on me, I would just smile at her. I was aware of the underlying pathos of life from a very young age. I believed my mother would experience some great sorrow and it was up to me to protect her. If she was not in the house when I came home from school, I would panic and think she had died.

I liked to watch butterflies, slaters and caterpillars; I liked to play dress up with my sisters. My little sister and I were ill a lot with bronchitis and we'd spend hours playing Monopoly, the board on the table between our beds. In my 20s, when I was working the late shift and living with a few flatmates who slept at night, I'd sit in my room and play Monopoly by myself, as four different people all with their own playing methods.

I was a keen reader from a very early age. I read everything – bus tickets, cereal packets, every book I could find. My parents couldn't afford a lot of books, but we got special ones for birthdays and Christmas, and we regularly went to the library. I had to get permission to read the older pupils' books at primary school, as I'd read all the ones for my age group. I tried to read while walking home but it didn't work. For a few years, I went through a phase of getting books out of the library and hand-copying the contents. I've always wished I could write out all the stories in my head and share them with those who'd like to read them.

Growing up, I desperately wanted to do ballet. I wrote my parents notes about it and put them under their pillows. They eventually found the money for this and I loved it. We would do a performance at the end of the year and my mother would make all the costumes for our class.

I loved being on stage, the curtains going back, the rosin on our shoes, the dressing up, the make-up. I never had stage fright, but I couldn't talk to the other students who'd often say nasty things to me after class. I don't think I could have been very good at ballet because of my clumsiness. I remember the teacher always telling me to smile. I've never liked smiling on cue. It makes everything seem so shallow. There is a such a deepness and mystery within our own unique facial expressions that putting our faces into a demanded pose seems to make light of this magnificence. My mother says I was born like an old woman, and now I am becoming one! Mind and body are starting to match.

Our family always had a lot of pets – cats, dog, guinea pigs and budgies. Cats would follow me home and I would always stop to speak to them. Even now, I acknowledge other species with more respect than most humans. I did try to fit in, though. When I went to intermediate school, I made the decision to become someone else, to become someone who could speak to other children. As it was a new school, I decided that it'd be a new start. I had three friends there, all smart kids, and we had a club called the Mirkwood club in which one had to read *The Hobbit* to join. You then had to write regular stories. We met under a large tree each week. I spent a lot of time with one of the girls in the club, Mary, who also had a vivid imagination like me. She wouldn't talk to me at school but at the end of the day she'd steal my bicycle from the bike stand and make a loud joke about it to anyone who might be listening, before riding off. I would ignore this and begin to walk to her place. She would meet me on the way and we'd either go to her house or mine.

I was useless at sports and didn't understand how people just knew how to play. I was the person left behind when teams were picked. They would argue over who was going to have to have me in their team. My PE teacher would change me from side to side in a game if she thought one side was winning too much. In the end, I just played four-square in a quiet playground with the fat girl, the stinky girl and the other odd girls like me.

Looking back, I wish I could say to myself, 'The aliens are not returning for you, so find your way in this world and trust yourself. You are different from most and that is great. Never diminish yourself to fit in. Camouflage is required at times for safety and harmony, but do not dull yourself or inhibit your imagination and intellect to appease. You are not broken!'

As it was, I eventually met the fascinating bad girl who had a ring with a small blade hidden in it. I followed the path of adventure and my studies became less important.

Much of the literature about Asperger's and high-functioning autism focuses on children, and I wonder how those kids will be when they grow up. In my childhood, I was ignorant of how my mind worked differently to other children's. Although it made life hard and confusing, it also made me resilient and put me in situations where I had to learn how to live in a neurotypical world. I learnt how to develop strategies to cope. I wonder whether excessive protection from the world will make it harder for this generation of high-functioning autistics.

Nowadays, there seem to be many pointless and destructive behaviours that humans do that are considered conventional. If I could change anything about the world, it would be that all humans would wake up one day and truly see the consequences of their behaviour. That they'd begin to act immediately to make things right, to care for our planet. I'd also make clothes for fellow uncomfortable people and I'd at long, long last learn to master the cello.

Steve

Electronics Expert

My current fascinations include abiogenesis, consciousness, evolutionary mechanisms, theoretical physics, astrophysics, astrobiology, electrostatics, amateur radio, mechanical engineering, optics, fencing, martial arts, historical sword-fighting, blacksmithing, floral arranging, cake decorating, ergonomic kitchen design, carpentry, programming, flint knapping, metallurgy, nuclear power, bookbinding, homebrewing of alcoholic beverages, paper marbling, welding, fiberglass, plastic and metal casting, airbrushing, paleontology, steam engines, internal and external combustion engines, building cars from scratch, anatomy, animal behavior and husbandry, plant splicing, electric motors and generators of all types and sizes, flying model airplanes, causes of mass extinctions, hydraulics, fluid flow, airplane engineering, clockmaking, geology, audio mixing and editing, video shooting, special effects, prop making, desktop publishing, digital photography, electrical wiring, hunting, tanning leather, knifemaking, science fiction, crime scene investigation, 3D printing, entomology, film developing and print making.

I have pale skin and a trimmed beard that used to be mahogany. My hair is auburn and somewhat neat, and I wear wireframe glasses.

My first alarm goes off at 4.30am. The second one an hour later stops me doing whatever I'm doing and reminds me to leave for work. I kiss my wife goodbye and pet our cats several times before leaving for work.

As I open the door, I brace myself. I was bullied a *lot* in middle school and high school. One of my former friends started a rumor that I was gay, which in the 1970s was the same as putting a target on my back. Older kids would ambush me on the way home, but I was very stoic when cornered. I wouldn't run; I'd just stand there waiting for them to get bored. When there was enough distance between us, I'd scoop up rocks and throw them. At my age, bullies are no longer so straightforward. But I am thinking about the possibility of a home invasion robbery every time I open the door. I don't walk around my van the same way every day. My eyes are up and looking around. I am mentally prepared to punch, kick, push or throw. I carry my keys, so I can stab an eye or throat. I've been told that when I'm walking, I often look like I'm on my way to kick someone's ass.

I've found a back way to get to work without ever going on the highway. Even though it takes a few more minutes, I have grown to really hate going on the highway. Speeding up and slowing down, cars cutting in front after passing on the right, it's all very stressful. The security guards make me nervous; I worry that I'm not giving the right amount of eye contact or the right facial expression.

I am a military contractor, repairing electronics for army training programs. Electronics is my vocation and my avocation.

I love fixing, designing and building things. The skills that the job requires are far below my abilities, but I'm being paid better than I have ever been before. I've repaired a large number of expensive items that had been deemed unrepairable. I've figured out new procedures for equipment that in the past was subject to constant complaints. I've built several jigs, fixtures and testers for all of us to use, and a few just for myself.

I joke around with my co-workers; we tease each other in the 'bro' way that neurotypical men do, insulting each other and making self-deprecating jokes. Although I had a hard time with this when I was young, taking it far too seriously, now it is one of my co-workers who will sometimes take a joking remark hard and get angry with me. I've never told them that I think I've got Asperger's, but I've not hidden it either. My boss once made the remark that I'm 'just like' his brother. His brother sounds like he's on the spectrum too.

My job before this one was building eddy current probes for finding cracks in metal. They're used a lot in airplanes and heat exchangers in powerplants. I loved the job. I made a lot of jigs and fixtures to make the job faster and more accurate. I also began repairing and maintaining the equipment we used. Unfortunately, it all came to an end when the owners moved operations to another location; only a few of us were asked to relocate.

On the bright side, this made me eligible for two years of free tuition and grants from the Displaced Worker Retraining Program. I went back to school to get an Electronic Engineering Associate of Technology degree. I took everything I could fit in. With permission, I sat in on classes I couldn't get credit for, because I wanted the knowledge. I started a student club and took part in student government, earned an extra scholarship for school supplies. I also finally took the tests to get my CET (Certified Electronic Technician) certificate, for both consumer electronics and computers, and certifications in soldering and soldering inspection. Oh, and I finally went for my ham radio license – passed all three tests in one evening!

My qualifications and experience enabled me to get my current job and it's great. But I'd be bored out of my skull if I couldn't listen to videos on topics of interest as I work.

Some days I might spend lunch with my co-workers. Other times, it seems like they wait until I've microwaved something first, but that's OK. I think most people can only stand just so much of my company. Break times, I mostly read. Or answer questions on Quora.

I always call my wife on my way home, using my bluetooth earpiece. I don't get lost in the conversation as I've seen others do; I'm the reverse. My attention automatically goes to traffic and I may even forget that I'm on the phone. I'll talk to my wife about thoughts I've had during the day, my thoughts on the videos I've listened to.

Sometimes I'm so deep in a conversation with her that I'll sit in the driveway for up to ten minutes before getting out the car. Once in, I hug and kiss my wife, pet and hug the cats (when they let me).

In the evenings we usually watch *NCIS* while eating dinner. In the past it was *Bones, Doc Martin* and *House*. I think I'm detecting a trend... Some nights I'll also try to get my electronics lab and workshop cleaned and organized; I have way too many projects started. I've just completed about a hundred; I've got about another hundred left.

One or two nights a week I teach at the local makerspace. I'm building the electronics bench there, and I've built and upgraded a small CNC carver. I like and dislike going. I want to be part of it, so I've learned to tolerate the noise and large number of people by being in kind of a bubble. The group seems heavy on people with Asperger's or ASD, diagnosed or not. I often feel cut out from what's going on. I've started the ball rolling on projects from which I've then been dis-included. People have volunteered to help me with programming projects, then just haven't shown up. I've seen my advice on a project ignored so many times. I realize some of this is due to them also being on the spectrum, but it's still frustrating and it still hurts.

I find it hard to sleep at night, so I have to make time to wind down. Sometimes I take a non-prescription sleep aid, sometimes I have some alcohol and sing along with music videos. My wife has strict instructions not to talk to me past this point. Even saying 'Goodnight' or 'I love you' is enough to get my brain spinning in circles.

As I get older, I'm getting so I don't want to be touched by anyone but my wife. I can no longer sleep in the same bed with anyone, not even the cats. I'm actually physically repulsed by unwelcome touching. I have a co-worker who in the past has thought it was funny to poke me in the belly as I walked past him. I told him twice to stop it, but he didn't, so I went to our boss. It stopped for a while but then about a month later he came up behind me and tickled my ribs. He did it *so* gently that I wasn't even sure I was being touched at first. It was the creepiest touch I've ever felt in my life.

When I was growing up, Asperger's was unknown to me, and autism was seen as mental retardation, kids slamming their heads repeatedly into a wall. When I told my sister (who has an autistic son and daughter) that I thought I had Asperger's, she said she already knew. I told a few select friends, and they all said things like 'Oh, I thought you knew'.

I know I'm weird, not because I feel that way, but because many people seem to find it necessary to tell me that. I think neurotypical people are weird too. They greet each other in a ritual manner, as if there is a script somewhere that was never given to me. I've had people I thought were friends stop talking to me, and when I've asked them why, they say it's because I don't ask them how they are. From experience, though, I can tell you that they don't want an honest answer. It sometimes feels like a 1960s spy movie where we're playing secret agents giving coded responses.

I remember as a child practicing facial expressions in the mirror. I noticed that while I was speaking, people would look bored and roll their eyes, so I also practiced speaking in a more engaging voice. I found it almost impossible to look people in the eye, though. It felt like a supernova going off. All the advice to stare at the forehead or nose did no good. I'd obsessively observe every pimple and pore, not hear a word that they said. I think I can read people's emotions quite well. The problem is, I think I can read way more than they mean to show. So someone says 'Good morning' with a smile. But I can see a tenseness around the corners of their mouth, a sadness in their eyes. Was it something I did? Should I ask if they're OK? Then I realize that they don't mean to show these emotions; they get angry if I give any sign that I've seen them. It's like trying to read a book printed on transparent pages. I can't tell the difference between the current page and what's supposed to be hidden deeper within.

I was a virgin and very lonely until I turned 27. I then learned I was incapable of completing the act of sex with someone I don't know and don't like. I had two attempts at one-night-stands but Mr Happy wasn't interested. I could get him up, but he'd lose interest too quickly to finish. Later I married my first wife and became very affectionate; making up for lost time, perhaps. She had fidelity problems, though, so our marriage didn't last very long.

I've been married to my second wife for 26 years. We still hug and kiss several times a day, and I tell her I love her a lot more than that. She used to ask me why I love her, but I've always found it hard to put it into words. We are very loyal to each other. When working around the house on my day off, sometimes I'll just go find my wife and hug her. Sometimes I cry when I'm hugging her, because I feel so overwhelmed. A couple of months ago, we were sitting having coffee and talking when a young woman in her 20s approached us to tell us that she and her boyfriend had been watching us, and that it made them feel really good watching us. That they could tell we clearly love each other very much. She asked how long we'd been together and said we looked like newlyweds.

I don't mean to make it sound like it's all butterflies and wine. We have arguments, we have problems. But we work at it. My wife is a wonderful, understanding woman, who is probably also on the spectrum. We have had very similar but not identical experiences. She was a fantastic kindergarten teacher (now retired) – great with kids, but not so good with adults.

Like I mentioned before, I was bullied a lot as I was growing up. When I was at school, I loved the idea of it but I didn't like the reality. It wasn't always just me that the bullies would pick on. Sometimes I'd have a friend who would get targeted instead.

I'd be ready to stand shoulder to shoulder, but every single one would run and leave me to face them alone. It wasn't till much later that I realized those that I thought of as friends only hung out with me when there was no one else.

Something that affected me greatly was an intelligence test we were given in sixth grade. Every parent had to sign a permission slip to allow their child to see the results. In the entire school, mine were the only parents who declined to let me see the results. But since I was one among hundreds, when they were calling names and handing out results, someone handed me mine. I had just enough time to read the raw numbers before someone snatched it back, chiding me as if I'd done something wrong.

I was devastated. There were several categories on the test. Because I was not supposed to see my results, no one explained them to me. So I thought it was an IQ test. I think the highest result was 98 or 99; others were numbers like 90, 70, 60, and one 50. I spent the rest of grade school and high school thinking I was below average. Every time a teacher drubbed me for not being correct, I'd think about that test and shut up. I only found out when my mother gave me a bunch of school stuff in my 40s that it was more like a percentile test. A score of 99 meant that, in that subject, I was above 99% of the population.

Fortunately, when I was by myself, I never thought of this. I spent a lot of my time reading instead. I was responsible for the local public library instituting a limit on the number of books that could be checked out at any one time. The head librarian didn't think I could be reading 15 at a time. But I was. I'd read when I woke up. I'd read to go to sleep. I'd go hiking, take a book, read for hours in the woods. I saw deer within

100 feet that didn't see me because I was so still while reading. So, because of the limit on books (six, I think), I'd just check out some books, then go in on a different day and make sure a different librarian was checking out books when I went up. One day, though, through a trick of circumstance, the same librarian that I'd checked out six books from the day before took over for the one checking out books just as I stepped up. I stood there nervously as she stamped the cards and put my information in. Then she leaned forward and whispered in my ear, 'You can check out as many books as you like.'

For most of grade school, I took everyone literally and at their word. I have large calcium deposits on each arm because I kept falling for the 'feather punch' game in sixth grade. The game, as told to me, was to hit each other on the arm lighter and lighter each time. So we'd take turns hitting each other on the shoulder lighter and lighter... Then suddenly the other boy would punch me hard on the arm and shout, 'You win!' I fell for it again and again. I thought I'd won and that they were just bad sports. Another kid had to tell me the point of the 'game' was to trick me into letting them hit me hard. The next day, I asked someone who'd done this to me many times if he wanted to try me at the 'feather hit' game again. When it came to the point where he punched me and shouted, 'You win,' I wound up and slammed him really hard on the shoulder and shouted back, 'No, YOU win!' I actually knocked him into a desk. He wanted to fight me; I asked, 'Over what? We played a game and you won!'

One day in high school, the so-called 'guidance counselor' called me in. This was weeks after all the other students' mandatory counseling sessions had ended. I seemed to be more of an afterthought, a box she had to check, reluctantly.

I remember her saying, 'High school is the best time of your life.' I told her that if she truly believed that, I'd just kill myself now. She asked me why I would say such a thing. So I told her. I told her about the highlights of my life, so far. The bullying for being smart and 'weird'. The rumors that had started in grade school that I was gay, that caused even adults in town to treat me like a diseased leper. The bullying by teachers and adults. I told her quite a lot. She seemed visibly shaken and told me that I *must* make an appointment to see her again the next day.

When I showed up the following morning, there were several members of staff waiting. A very large man loomed over me, demanding to know what I'd said to my counselor, whom I could hear crying in the back office. I told him and the other adults that I'd just answered her questions about why I'd want to kill myself. I was told that I was lying about what I'd said to her. She took a year off as a result of this and I was assigned to a 6 foot 5 male counsellor who handled all the tough cases, the ones that were on their way to prison if someone didn't intervene. I never did get any useful career counseling.

I started thinking a lot about suicide after that. At one point, I laid down in the snow in the small hours of the morning in my underwear. I figured I'd be cold for a while, then feel warm and fall asleep. I was found before that happened. My parents had heard the back door, I guess. My father came out and told me to come back in the house. It was never to be mentioned again.

In my early 20s, failing out of US Navy Nuke School, I put a hose in my tailpipe and started the car. I started thinking, though, about the baby my sister had just had. What would he think when he got older and asked about me? I took the hose out and went AWOL instead.

I had several other times when I just felt so miserable and desperately lonely that I thought about ending my life. What would save me, though, would be the realization that the universe is just so darn interesting!

Frank

Childcare Worker

I'm a man in my 50s, recently diagnosed. I'm 5 foot 7, of average build with long grey hair that used to be blond. I have a trimmed moustache, a beard and blue eyes. I'm an antitheist, a poet and a pro-life liberal.

I grew up in Germany where I found the social rules and exceptions very confusing. To me, they were a labyrinth of awkwardness. In Germany, strangers (unless both are young and meet informally), formal contacts (such as colleagues, teachers, waiters, shop assistants, etc.) and authorities are addressed in the plural ('Sie') instead of the singular ('Du'), besides using Mr/Mrs. Here in Ireland, at least in my experience, everybody is addressed by their first name with the exception of doctors and clerics (and occasionally in written correspondence with businesses, agencies, etc., when one doesn't know the addressee personally). This makes things a lot easier. Also, in Ireland, one is more likely to be approached by others. For someone who very rarely takes the initiative for fear of imposing on others, this provides more chances to meet people. Ireland is more informal in many ways, but the 'old boy network' is a lot stronger (or at least more obvious) here than it is in Germany. One peculiar habit, which took me time to adjust to, was being greeted with 'How are you?' by people who wouldn't wait for a reply. It took me five years to get used to it, another five years to do it myself.

I currently live on my own in a rented two-bedroom house on the outskirts of town. While stress and anxiety used to be a crippling part of my life, all this changed when my disability allowance was approved. (I have to add that I don't see myself disabled by my autism; I see myself as disabled by society.) Although I still try to find work as a childcare worker (at which I am brilliant, according to former employers, colleagues, parents and children), I am no longer under pressure from the unemployment office. This new-found absence of anxiety allows me to focus on my literary work without being distracted by worries. The free public transport provided by my disability allowance also helps me get out of the house in the warmer months. It enables me to hike and take landscape photos for my website.

Day to day, though, I tend to be found in my study (the second bedroom), composing traditional poems (i.e. with metre and rhyme), studying topics of interest, writing articles for my website and applying to every local childcare position available. Even though autistic people tend to be excellent in their chosen professions, 85% of us are unemployed and, as a childcare worker in Ireland, being autistic is one obstacle, being male another. Time in front of the laptop is broken up by toast, microwave meals and the occasional film in the sitting room. Sometimes my concentration is broken by barking dogs in the neighbourhood. If this is the case, I blow my dog whistle until they stop. Around 8.30pm I watch a horror film with a few glasses of wine. The film serves as a distraction; it helps me to wind down.

Over the past few years I've come to realise that I don't really need to socialise. My only regular interactions are in a weekly poetry circle and a monthly open mic (followed by a visit to the pub). That's enough for me. Occasionally, I meet a family who avail themselves of my free 'autism mediation service'. I help the parents get a better understanding of their autistic children, and I help their children to relate more to the world around them.

Jacqueline

Human

When I was 27, I went to a new-age workshop looking for answers. The convener directed us to remember a time we were happy and content, a time of peace, a time without fear or anxiety. I couldn't remember one – couldn't find a time without fear or sadness or anxiety or pain. Not one.

I don't think it was because I didn't have times of joy as a younger person. Rather, my experiences held so many fears, so much overwhelm, that I could not (and still struggle to) remember the joys of my childhood.

Here I am in my 50s, though, and finally I can say I am happy. I don't think I would have learned how to feel this way without the identification of my autism in my 40s. I have learned what contentment, love and joy feel like for me, and I'm lucky enough to experience them every day. It certainly makes the ongoing overwhelm, overload and anxiety of everyday life easier to deal with.

Back when I was a child, I was molested by a family friend. I subsequently entered many unhealthy relationships throughout my teens and 20s. I hadn't yet learned how to say no to someone, or even to examine myself and my needs enough to differentiate them from those of another. I had learned, unfortunately, to deny my inherent gut instincts about people.

My (pen)ultimate solution in my 30s was to stay out of relationships. I learned to be truly content as a single. I made friends, just a few friends, but good friends, lifelong friends. I thought I'd continue life alone but not lonely, right through into my retirement years.

I never expected to fall in love again. In my 50s. With a man over 5000 miles away. But that's exactly what happened just a few years ago. We've been married now just over a year. Neither of us have been married before. He also has Asperger's. I'd shared a description of my latest meltdown on a social site and he 'liked' it. Conversation ensued.

Our long-distance dialog led to a 'first date'. We met halfway. This led to more travel, a proposal. And then the biggest move of my life. From a beachside resort town in the subtropics to a wooded acreage in the snow belt. Life since the move hasn't become any simpler, but it has become even happier.

I'm enjoying exploring my new landscape here. I experience the world through exquisite sound, sight and tactile sensitivity, can feel physical sensations from seeing beauty; some say it is a kind of synesthesia. I can get a physical rush and I will often form tears. Falling snow sparkling in the moonlight. The beauty of walking through a drifting fog. A daffodil peeking up through the snow. The heat of a tropical sun against my skin. Walking barefoot across warm, rough rocks.

It gets very cold here. Last winter, I was the coldest I've ever been. It got to around –15°C. We went to the edge of a frozen lake; I'd never seen anything like it before. The sand and water had formed into solid waves; ice stretched beyond the horizon. The snow was like tiny floating grains of sand. I stood on a planet I've known for 50 years and felt like I was in a new world. The global sensory experience was incredible – visual and tactile newness everywhere. I was jumping on my toes with glee as my tears of amazement froze on my cheeks.

To a random observer, I would have seemed odd, I am sure; it was the kind of behavior I had learned to curb in order to fit in, to endure a life surrounded by people who don't feel the world the way that I do. My husband, he grinned to see my reaction. He loves the excitement I feel at nature's wonder; not only does it allow him to see his familiar environment anew, but it enables him to lead me to something that gets me out of masking and into pure sensory experience. He is a wonder, just like that ice-scape was.

I am lucky to be able to use my joy and wonder in nature as a calming 'stim'. It seems to help stabilize and manage the sensory and cognitive overload that comes hand in hand with my autism.

I also use physical motions like swaying gently when standing still (coincidentally, my husband sways at the same rate as I do), or spending hours jumping or diving through rolling waves. Even getting into a sweat in the garden with hard physical work can help to get my system equalized.

Interestingly, it is not just nature that can give me the visual beauty chills that feel so good. The built environment, food, color, design, pretty much all the 'things' in life – they all seem to have either a positive or negative effect on my body and spirit. It is more intense than a preference or a liking for something. Bright colors can give me a burst of joy; beige or muted tones seem to dampen my spirits, and sometimes they make me physically nauseous.

Of course, I can't avoid all the pitfalls of life. I work too much, I shop and do dishes. I cook, and I speak to strangers on the phone. I have a list of chores that grows longer each day and sometimes the pressure of getting life lived turns a joyful activity into an anxiety-provoking chore.

Also, I still have meltdowns. It's been a challenge for me to accept that I will probably never not have meltdowns. I have developed so many great strategies for equilibrating my neurology, though. Some of these I learned before my diagnosis. Those people side-eying me in traffic, for example, because my music is so loud and my out-of-tune singing is disturbing their mobile call – they have no idea that singing at the top of my lungs while I drive enables me to let go of the pent-up energy or distress.

Some strategies I have developed consciously since my diagnosis, through working with some incredible people (shout-out to Tony and Michelle). I have learned to develop a supportive inner voice rather than berating myself for who I am and how I sometimes behave.

I rarely meltdown in public – I usually have an escape plan these days if I know I'm entering a stressful situation. And I seem to have developed an innate strategy where I leak out my reactions in tears if I cannot escape, somehow holding off the rampage till I can let go in private. So a lot of people have seen me cry (a lot) in various situations, but few people have ever seen me meltdown as an adult. My father once, I think, my mother a few times, and my husband.

The times with my mother, I remember seeing her crying, watching helplessly as I careened in agony. She didn't really understand; she desperately wanted to help but she didn't know how. I recognize that she feels responsible somehow. I hope one day she will know that it is not her fault – this is how I am, and I love being who I am, even with the additional challenges that I have.

The first meltdown in front of my husband was one of the hardest things I've ever been through. Even though we had met through my description of a meltdown, and he'd supported me over the phone during and after them, I was plain terrified that he wouldn't be able to cope seeing me curl into a ball of frustration, screams and terror, before returning back to our adult relationship. I thought that somehow it would change how he felt about me. But...I picked the right guy! He was (as he always is) incredible. He seems to know instinctively what to do. Always. He holds me, tight. Sometimes we rock together. He'll also help me apply pressure to my head (to avoid me punching or knocking myself). He tells me he loves me, but mostly he does not speak. It breaks him up inside to see me like that, I know it does. So I will continue to practice every strategy I can to keep my neurology stable, to avoid putting him through more meltdowns. I think he is more distressed by them than I am.

I'm not sure what my future holds; thinking of the future is challenging for any autistic person. I am up for the challenge, though. And my husband is with me. We may just have to work a bit harder at it than most. We are the hidden autistics. The invisible ones. The late-diagnosed and the undiagnosed. We're here, but largely unaccounted for because we 'cope'. We find a way to make our way, with little to no support for our varied needs. Few people ever see through our public presentation to the real 'us'. But we know each other, my husband and me. To know and be known, isn't that what most of us really want? We have that, and it is enough. Actually, it's more than enough. It is everything.

Tony

Athletic Husband

It was being a volunteer firefighter that got me into athletics. I'd started going to the competitions between the different brigades when I realised I was a bit slow with my running. I took to the track to get my speed up, and before long I was totally hooked.

I live in a city, 90 miles from Melbourne. There's about 100,000 people in total. It used to be used for mining, so there's a lot of really good 19th-century architecture. Despite it being built-up, it's only five minutes from open bushland. It's typical Australia. Open forest, not a lot of undergrowth; eucalyptus trees and kangaroos. In fact, there's usually a whole mob of roos in the next paddock to where I train.

I live here with my husband, our cat, our dog and our rabbit. I met my husband online with no intentions, both just looking for friendship. It was love at first sight. Literally. We've been together now 13 years. Got married earlier this year. With all the law changes, it finally happened. He's on the spectrum too (we established this early on). He's the creative one; he likes crafts, costume making, reading comics, that kind of thing. We've a lot in common too. For example, we're both really into science fiction and each night after dinner we watch a series such as *Star Trek, Stargate, Land of the Lost*. We've seen every episode of *Doctor Who* three times, right through from the first episodes back in the 1960s to the modern day. We tend to like a lot of the British stuff in general, especially drama. There are good scriptwriters in Britain and I think that the Australian way of doing things is fairly similar.

Most of my days are pretty varied, but they always include one or two track or field sessions that carry on through into the evening. I'm a bit of a tech geek, so I tend to use Mondays to focus in on this. Tuesdays usually find me at the end of a shovel or a wheelbarrow, carrying out gardening and grounds maintenance at a local school. Wednesdays are for errands, Thursdays for yoga. Fridays can be anything, whilst Saturday is always sports day (track or cross-country). On Sundays you'll find me at the fire station.

I've always done quite a bit of volunteering in my community. Up until recently I was running an autistic youth programme using technology as an aid for social interaction. It was very unstructured; it helped teenagers to pursue their own interests. I often run various fundraisers for local causes that support autistic youth and adults, and I've spoken at autistic conferences on topics such as sexuality and the benefits of participating in sports. A lot of people now know me because of all this; I think people are more willing to listen nowadays.

What's in my head tends to be very different to how I actually speak. The structure and grammar are like nothing I've ever seen in print. There are multiple dimensions, always at least four, and concepts such as time are ever-changing. My thought processes consist of symbols; they're not linear. Everything is constantly in flux. It can become pretty tiring just trying to get the words out, because there are so many lined up ready to create the strings of conversation.

I was first diagnosed in my early 20s. I was with my first partner at the time; he was the one who noticed it. It was called Asperger's back then. I was actually the first openly gay autistic person on the internet; I had a website that's still running today. I was also one of the founding board members of ASAN (Autistic Self Advocacy Network) of Australia and New Zealand.

They call having a diagnosis here a kind of functional impairment. I'm currently undergoing re-diagnosis for access to the national disability insurance scheme (although the government are looking to tighten up the criteria/wording for it as it's currently flooded with autistic people). The idea behind the scheme is to improve access and participation in society. Gaining access would give me personalised support. I'd be allocated a planning meeting to talk about life goals, desires, that kind of thing. They'd then create a plan which would include funding to support me. I haven't gotten to that stage yet. Right now, the disability employment agency is helping me pay for the psychologist part of the assessment, but I might need to look at other ways to fund the occupational therapy component. The whole process has taken over a year so far; it's become a bit of an experience, a bit of an adventure.

Indigo

Chameleon

My husband and I met in our teens. We've been married now for 24 years, a couple for 34. He was the first person who I felt loved me unconditionally. We're very different but we share the same core values. We've raised two amazingly successful and yet equally opposite kids, and although we haven't the most harmonious marriage, we work it out. A deep abiding love has always connected us, carried us though all our personal challenges.

It's three years now since a flood destroyed our home. It's all very vivid: six feet of water on the only roads out by 10am. Our neighbors (whose son I taught) lived on the banks of a pond in an elevated home. The water was rising from the river fast and making roaring rapids not far from their door, so they came to stay with us. I'm physically challenged by psoriatic arthritis and fibromyalgia, and our house had always been a pile of endless clutter. Having people in my space, seeing my mess – that was hard.

It was a dark noisy night, no electricity. Things falling over and moving about beneath us. We heard air boats going back and forth on the road behind our house, rescuing people from single-story homes. A van's alarm sounded on the street, its headlights flashing under the water till its battery stopped dead. The wife of our neighbor was diabetic with an insulin pump that kept beeping 'beep-beep'. We'd adopted a kitten and our old cat still wasn't used to her; they had to be separated, kept from running downstairs. Luckily, we had two cat carriers.

At dawn we used the only phone with power to call for rescue. A boat came up to our door and we waded out. The neighbor's wife was crying, but I was numb. We were deposited on dry land and found my son's friend. I asked them for a ride to my husband's aunt's place. My mother-in-law and sister-in-law were already there.

As the days went on, it became very evident that the people who were doing better emotionally, mentally and even physically were those that had strong relationships with friends and family. My son's friends were significant; several helped muck out our house. I'd failed miserably at keeping friends, but I did have one I could rely on. That one sent us a contractor when there seemed to be none. It was then that I realized I couldn't go on keeping to myself.

And yet I still found it hard to form bonds with people. I remember coming home from school to a gutted first floor; no neighbors were back. I'd try to sneak past the Spanish-speaking sub-contractor and his wife, as I knew they wanted me to be happy at the progress, but I just couldn't fake it. I became unable to regulate my sensory issues, became overwhelmed by sounds, lights and smells. I had massive anxiety just being awake. After about a month, I sought help for sensory processing disorder. I saw an OT (occupational therapist) and started calming and mitigating strategies. I took one day at a time.

It wasn't until I was alone in an empty, quiet house that I realized sensory issues didn't answer all my questions. I wasn't facing sensory issues every day. I'd quit working, had entire days of solitude, yet still I had meltdowns. I took myself to a testing psychologist and was, at the age of 51, diagnosed ASD level 1 with executive functioning issues (ADHD). The psychologist said that if I hadn't had the ability to describe in detail my history of interpersonal social struggles, he wouldn't have seen the autism at all.

I've always battled with feelings that I don't really fit in anywhere. Up until the diagnosis, my whole life had been spent going through the motions, making major life decisions based on my perception of other people's expectations. Trying to follow my own heart and mind met with so much resistance, and I seldom had enough determination to withstand the discouragement. I'd been to art school, found a teaching job, got married, had kids, found a life path that seemed to suit me well. But it all was a struggle. A hidden, horrifying, gut-wrenching struggle. And only ever when I tried to engage with the world, with people. I failed, got back up, tried something else, failed again. Before the diagnosis, I didn't feel like I'd ever succeeded. Yet from outward appearances I'd accomplished quite a lot.

The diagnosis therefore was life-changing; it made everything fall into place. I'm now learning more and more about myself every day. For example, during a recent visit to my therapist I realized that what she believes I am saying and what is my intent to express are actually two different things. She thinks I've said I'm feeling sad when I've meant to say I'm wistful and reflective yet accepting. It's not the same as sadness; sadness is too simple. I realize then that it's always been this way: others believing I've said one thing, but me believing I've said something very different. Also, when I'm observing things, describing how they are, people think I'm complaining. They think I'm unhappy about whatever it is, when I'm really not. Somehow my tone doesn't convey my meaning. It's a matter of perspective, I guess. How one person saying 'It's bright in here' could mean it's cheery and light, but it could also mean their eyes hurt from it.

I'm more aware now as well of my habit of misremembering feelings from the past. Most memories of vacations evoke the worst thing that happened. Happy memories are much harder to formulate and hold on to. So last year, when redecorating our home, I decided our bedroom walls would be like a scrapbook. With photographs of holidays and outings, interspersed with souvenir magnets we've collected. As well as a wall for our family trips, I have one called 'been there & done that'. That wall's for my kids' adventures. My daughter has traveled a lot since leaving home: Canada, China, Belize, Israel, Iceland. And my son drove across country last summer. Doing the walls like this means that the photos of our family holidays bring back the bright happy moments that I was part of, whereas the ones from my kids' trips remind me that they are on their own adventures now. So it's playing to my visual thinking; it's helping my emotional understanding and recall. When I wonder what I've done with my life, it's all right there. I look up at it and think, 'I did that. And it was good.'

Herman
Historian

At this stage of my life, I'm a fairly rotund figure with a full grey beard. I used to dream of being a Cistercian monk, but then I realised it'd involve more celibacy than I was prepared for.

I've been married twice now and I love my wife dearly, but there's one point that has the potential to harm us, and that is order. I need it in my life for everything that I do, whereas my wife lives all higgledy-piggledy. Clothes, the dishwasher, spices in the rack; everything has to be in the right place at all times. Only then can the correct tools be chosen for the task in hand. The simple affair of hanging a picture, for example. I tend to become absorbed in close communication with the toolbox, selecting the proper nail size, the right hammer, spirit level, sharpened pencil to mark *The Place*. By the time I emerge, fully kitted out for the job, my wife has found an old nail in a drawer and gone on to hammer it in with the heel of her slipper...

My mother, a secondary school teacher of biology, chemistry and geography, also married twice. She was a hard, strong woman. Her first husband was a secondary school teacher too. My birth coincided with their divorce, following on from an illicit relationship with yet another secondary school teacher. She later married this second man and always stated that I was his son.

My mother returned to school six weeks after my birth, so my maternal grandmother did much of my upbringing. She'd suffered severe trauma from the war and was apt to run down into cellars whenever she heard an aircraft. We were living in the vicinity of a military airbase and international airport at the time.

My grandmother found me an extremely precocious child. She delighted in giving me what she called the foundations of life. She found nothing unusual in a child of two reading fairy tales on his own. Someone else, however, thought that quite remarkable: a nun in the Order of St Mary Ward, a secondary school teacher and a qualified psychologist. She was the one chosen to look after me whenever my grandmother was at her job in the post office. From what I gather, she mentioned to my mother that I was different from other kids – that it might be worth getting me assessed by a psychiatrist. My mother strongly resented this idea and cut contact with her immediately. Whenever I asked for my 'black-and-white auntie', I was first fobbed off with the information that she had been transferred to a far distant monastery, and later that she'd passed away.

Soon after, I started attending the local Catholic kindergarten. It was a shock as I'd never been in contact with other kids. Now there was a roaring mass of around 50 of them, sketchily supervised by two teachers. After causing a fight (I took the wheels from another boy to complete my Lego aircraft), it was decided I should have my own small table in a remote corner so as not to bother the others. I saw this as a reward, because now I was more or less free from attending all those silly kindergarten games. Instead, I was allowed to play or draw (mostly draw) on my own. I didn't manage to draw creatively, but I did draw circles. Large circles in all available colours, nice and concentric. And accurate. As if they had been drawn with a compass.

If they'd just left me alone, I could have survived kindergarten quite easily. But every so often the kindergarten teachers changed, sometimes three or four times a year. And the new ones, not knowing anything about me, tried to get that 'poor lonely boy' involved. It always ended with catastrophic results.

It wasn't long before I started resisting going to kindergarten, rolling on the floor, kicking and struggling. There was never any investigation into why I was reacting this way; I was just a recalcitrant malefactor to be dealt with. My grandfather took to wrapping me in a horribly scratchy grey woollen blanket until I was just a heaving bundle. He'd carry me to kindergarten, push me inside the door and hold it shut until the teacher dragged me away. I spent many days crying my heart out, staring at my grandfather's receding figure.

The bullies spotted me on the first day at primary school. One of their favourite pranks was to snatch my glasses and either hide or break them. When that novelty wore off, they started punching me. Their final zenith of cruelty was to fall on me as a group of six or seven and drag me behind one of the clumps of bushes. They'd take turns to hold me down as the leaders practised their football kicks on me, concentrating on my...well, balls. Because that evoked the most satisfying cries of pain. The result of all this was urinary tract damage that required surgery. I had almost constant blunt testicular trauma and, as an adult, was left completely infertile.

My mother was asked to see the principal several times about it. As before, she stonewalled every attempt at getting me professionally assessed, and even the teacher's statement that I was being violently bullied did not get her to relent. In fact, her only reaction to their attempts at helping me was to complain to the education authorities and get them into trouble. The teachers therefore washed their hands of the matter and took to serenely ignoring me instead.

While my mother was alive, she always, and consistently, whenever I asked about my father, gave this answer: 'I was in love with your father, my second husband, but my parents didn't approve as he was still a student. My first husband had already been instituted as a teacher, and was a permanent civil servant. My parents therefore forced him upon me. I loathed him for that and for being a monster and a psychopath. This is what forced me into my love affair with my second husband. My first husband never had any interest in you. Shortly after the divorce, he was judicially confined in a psychiatric institution and died there within a year or two.'

I believed her, as you do. When she contracted Alzheimer's disease and ensuing dementia, I became her carer and plenipotentiary. And, during one period when she was confined to a gerontopsychiatric ward after trying to attack me with a paper knife, I found a big file full of old papers. Inside was every scrap of writing connected to her divorce and remarriage.

As in the case of my 'black-and-white auntie', everything she had ever told me was one well-thought-out circumstantial lie. Her first marriage undeniably was a marriage for love, after a long and blissful engagement. However, my mother always had an insatiate greed for money, and when another, more prosperous guy appeared, even though he was married and had a daughter, she quickly transferred her affections to him.

Her first husband was done out of home and family but, far from being a monster and psychopath confined to an institution, he turned out to be a sentimental, soft-hearted, shy man who went on to become vice principal of a secondary school, married again and only passed away some 20 years later, more or less from a broken heart, at the all-too-early age of 60.

Far from being not interested in me, his letters during the divorce proceedings are teeming with 'I don't care what happens to me as long as everything is good for the child'. Every weekend, for years on end, he drove more than 120 miles in the hope of catching just a glimpse of me. When I finally unearthed a few of his colleagues and former students, all of them were unanimous in attesting to his shy and withdrawn character, as well as his inordinate passion for music and history. They spoke of his love of detail and immense knowledge, his powers of observation and his talent for telling stories which seamlessly followed each other. They told me about his taking customary sayings and puns at their full face value and his strong aversion to change. When they told me that he always insisted on each item of a student's kit being in its appointed place at all times, I knew that, unknowingly, he had been on the spectrum as well...and that he must have been my father, as he himself never doubted.

Dave
Magus

As a child, I didn't find that my peers gave me the mental stimulation I needed. They weren't interesting enough to hold my attention; my mind would just go off exploring by itself. I was content with my own company and didn't need the validation of other children anyway. I don't know if my peers thought I was a little strange (aren't we all really?), but my real friends weren't concerned in the least. Why? Because they lived in a small box in the lounge. They were my friends, my mentors, my peeps; the ones that I most related to. Especially the captain of the *USS Enterprise*. At the age of eight or nine, I also found myself constantly embattled by Kirk's split personality disorder (now known as dissociative identity disorder). If a dilemma presented itself (either on the show or in real life), I would all too frequently take the logical high ground of Spock. The most frustrating part of this was not understanding why the logical conclusion didn't always work, but how McCoy's emotional side of Kirk seemed to defy logic. I spent many an hour trying to figure this out. Subsequently, 'Let it go' was a term I often heard growing up. But I was stuck to it like flypaper, and it had hold of me. I couldn't let it go as it wouldn't let me go. Round and round in my mind we went.

In the early days of my relationship with my wife, she would often say, 'Yes, Mr Spock', as I embodied Spock when favouring the logical part of my brain (and really why wouldn't I?). Unfortunately, she forgot at some point in our relationship that the 'Mr Spock' aspect of me was very definitely a part of who I am. It came to annoy her, particularly when she had planned a special event or celebration and I didn't get excited about it, much to her disgust.

As I had grown up into adulthood, I had become less inclined to socialize. I didn't follow my peers into the time-honoured tradition of every night at the pub/bar or weekend parties that actually lasted the full weekend. That just wasn't part of who I was. I told myself that I didn't need those things in my life, but, looking back, I realise I was actually full of anxiety at the thought of being around too many people that I didn't know. Or want to know, for that matter. If I hadn't successfully managed to manoeuvre my way out of avoiding a social occasion, I would reluctantly attend and be the one in the corner of the room ever so slightly distant from everyone else. I didn't see this as abnormal at all, as I'd been told by adults that I was shy. Really shy. They were wrong, though. I wasn't just shy. The Maori word for it is a far less limiting descriptor: 'Whakama'. It means bashful. Embarrassed. Ashamed. Shy and so, so much more.

My late teens to late 30s was all spent learning how to engage socially with other people. I observed social interactions from a distance. I watched guys speak confidently to girls, but I didn't have the confidence to do it myself. It wasn't something that came naturally or easily, but I worked at it. Other people rolled with it, but for me it was as if someone had tied my shoes together in the playground: step, trip, stumble, get up and repeat.

At one point I reasoned that all I had to do was 'Just do it', as the advertising campaign goes. So I applied for a job through a contact of a contact (it wasn't 'what' but 'who' you knew) as a sales consultant. Huge mistake. After six months the boss called me into his office, made me an offer. I didn't realise that I was being pitched a sales offer. He promptly let me go. My confidence plummeted over the subsequent years. Depression made me feel a complete outcast. Five years later, I journeyed into the job world once more, to try my luck again.

Over the following ten years I had a series of dead-end jobs. Each one took me a step closer to my dream job. From the age of five or so, I had dreamed of being on the radio and one day (after 20 years of trying and failing) I found the courage to apply. By sheer luck, I landed a part-time gig with a newly launching nationwide oldies format station. You might wonder why anyone with a social disorder would put themselves so far out there as to do radio? But being on the air was always the goal and being behind a microphone was not out in public; I didn't have to see my audience. This was probably the best period of my life (excluding times with my wife, daughter, mother and my best friend, Toby the dog). There were still times where it went pear-shaped, but it always worked out in the end. Now, with my training as a counsellor, I have learned that I *can* learn, that I *can* connect with others in a meaningful way. The only down-side I've discovered is that my cigarette habit is exacerbated when I'm anxious, and I'm anxious when I have new clients or am involved in difficult social situations. Smoking has replaced the need to chew on something; without the cigarettes, it would be my lips or my tongue.

I do an awful lot of thinking now outside of the box; I suppose I always have done. An awful lot of reflecting, self-reflecting. If there was one thing that school taught me, it was that I was stupid. Just because my thoughts were different. I believed what they said until I proved them wrong. Do I think like the rest of the world? I don't really know. What does the rest of the world think like?

Giovanni

Engineer

I'm a cis-male. Part Cherokee, part Scot, part Italian. I'm 6 foot 4 and weigh in at 230 pounds. I have long graying black hair, intense brown eyes and a van-Dyke beard. I'm more muscular than most, but not bodybuilder standard. I have a general battle/workworn look about me, but a look of kindness as well. Many people instinctively trust me just because of my appearance.

My age is starting to become a thing for me now. Although I'm generally in better health than I was in my 20s (well, physically stronger at least), I'm finding that my memory for what I perceive to be trivial information is fading. I can remember how to do things and I seem to retain my magic ability to learn whatever I want, and my intuitive understanding about how things work, but I just feel, slow, demotivated, lazy even. I'm worried for my finances, and even more so for my future. I feel constantly stressed to do something more than I am doing, to earn more, to be more, to spend more time with my family.

Over the years I've carefully avoided any autism diagnosis

for fear of what it will do for my future career options. I believe that much of what I want to do with my life would be precluded by a diagnosis. Apart from the nerd or tech community, I've found society to basically fear, ridicule or treat autistic people with pity. I don't want that. I've had a lot of clinical depression over the years, again not officially diagnosed for the same reason. For a while I visited a psychiatrist who treated me off the record. I found that very useful.

I'm currently in a polyamorous relationship with a teacher, but neither of us is actively involved with anyone else. She's on maternity leave right now. She's on the high-functioning side of the spectrum – what we used to call Asperger's. We know how to deal with each other's shit, and that is what keeps us together. We do like each other, and we do love each other, but we are basically in a sexless relationship. She has a lack of desire. It may be her autism, a co-morbid condition or something unrelated. It may simply be that she doesn't find me attractive. Whatever the reason, it causes me a lot of frustration and self-doubt. It ruins my confidence and it makes me depressed. Right now, our relationship seems mostly to revolve around making and raising children. I'm no longer successful when seeking other relationships, and I rarely even look.

I don't have typical days. I work for myself. Kind of... I basically pick up whatever contract or gig I can get. Often it's construction work, for which my alarm (which is set to seagull sounds) goes off at 6.10am. I have to be careful getting out of bed because our three-year-old girl still sleeps with us. I usually wake tired, after having been kicked or forced into a cramped position by her. I try to have left my clothes out in the hallway the night before so as not to wake anyone else. Depending on how tired or horny I am, I'll take a shower, pick up my clothes, get dressed once I'm downstairs.

In the kitchen, the first thing I do is ask Alexa for the daily news and then, because of a ridiculous acid reflux condition, I have a cup or two of fennel, ginger, lemon and turmeric 'tea'; it seems to help with my stomach. I tend to eat a lot of protein for breakfast, and I'm usually out the door before anyone else wakes up.

When I'm working on construction jobs, I face the site with dread. I often feel like an outcast. Nine times out of ten, I'm proved wrong but the dread's still there when I turn up. I tend to work harder (i.e. longer) than most, in part due to the feeling of being an imposter. I try to follow the existing break and lunch schedules, but I often don't want to break and so keep on working. Or I just plain miss that others are taking a break. I have a tough time reading others, so I really have no idea how well I'm doing, except that they just keep calling me back. When they finally don't, I spend days agonizing over what I did wrong and how can I fix it next time. Even though I have no real evidence that performance was anything to do with it.

On days that I don't do construction, and I'm working on my own things around the house, my day starts the same, except that I am usually woken by one of my two children and I'll often make breakfast for them. Then I do whatever task needs to be done such as paperwork or whatever task my co-star has set me while she's at work. If I have enough time after that, I'll do something for me, such as online classes I'm trying to take; learning something new makes me happy. That 'aha' moment of realization and understanding.

In the evening I usually end up on kid duty till bedtime. The four-month-old falls asleep readily, but we have to start putting our daughter to bed an hour before bedtime. She's already showing some signs of being on the high-functioning end of the spectrum. Lately, she's become a daddy's girl and I have to go to bed with her to get her off to sleep. If I don't do this and try to get on with some work, she comes in and disrupts everything she can get her hands on. We'd like to have at least one more child; a total of four would be good.

During my lifetime, I've traveled some in North America. From the Mexican Riviera to the High Canadian Arctic, from −55°F to 80°F, from Florida to California, from 86m below sea level on land (and nearly the same underwater) to 4400m above. I've worked as a carpenter, plumber, electrician and roofer. I've served in the military as a tow-truck driver, EMT (emergency medical technician), firefighter, marine contractor/commercial diver, mechanic, welder, mountaineering and survival instructor, as an electronics, computer and network technician. I've acted on stage and in movies, and I've worked in TV. I've studied (but rarely graduated) as a mechanical engineer and commercial pilot. I've triple-majored in engineering physics, computer science and electrical engineering, and I hold several professional certificates. I used to be well known in the New Space community, and I've led several analog (simulated) space missions. I'm the only person I know who's done everything on Robert Heinlein's 'Competent Person' list and I've given so many talks that I can't remember them all. I've had many people cheer at the mere mention of my name, yet I'm still not sure I've done anything important. Most people, I guess, list children as an important 'thing they've done', but I just don't see that I've had much to do with it except as a genetic donor. Maybe a bit in raising and teaching them, but I'm afraid I'm screwing my daughter up, and I'll probably do the same to my son when he's older. Over the years, I've had ideas and inventions taken from me, businesses and reputation, my self-respect and my respect from others. I've lived through a house fire and I've lost many family members, including my brother. I'm just carrying around so much pain and frustration right now. It comes out as anger, but I'm not an angry person, not really. I think very highly of myself, but I hate myself at the same time. I feel like most of what I do is meaningless. What I want to do is get funding to use tech to help people, to make their lives easier. I want to make us a space-faring race. I want to make the dreams of science fiction a reality.

Our 60s

Maggie

Dreamer

I've been medically retired now for four years. I used to work for the secret service but then I got severe dilated cardiomyopathy. It's got a lot worse recently, so I'm on an experimental drug. It has a lot of interesting side effects. I was told not to Google it but unfortunately I did.

Some days I'm all right; I can go out with my designated driver and my blue badge. Other days I'm pretty wiped out and am pretty much housebound. Right now, I get out a few times a week.

I always cut off from everybody at six o'clock at night. I need that space to basically just recharge. If someone tries to contact me after that time, I go a bit into panic mode and can't answer. Unless, of course, they've chopped their leg off or something.

I live near the beach in a flat. I've got a few incredibly close friends who've known me for years. They've always known I'm a bit nutty, always known I come out with weird stuff and don't get jokes. I have face blindness too, which can cause a lot of laughs. I can be out in the street and I'll walk straight past one of them. I'll get a text a little while later saying, 'You just walked straight past me', and I'm like, 'Oh no, not again!' I've done it to my daughter too.

Also, I have this strange thing where if I use a toilet in a public place, I need someone I know waiting outside. Because I'll come out and I won't know where I am. It can be really scary. Something that's always helped in situations like that, though, is to do maths in my head; the numbers help calm me.

Out the window of my flat, all I can see are trees and cliffs and fields. It's a bit of a building site at the moment as they're re-doing the outside and the communal areas. It's not too bad as they gave a lot of warning. The estate owner knows I have Asperger's and knows that I'm not well. They've all been very good to me and it'll look lovely when it's done.

I grew up in a really small, rich area; spent a lot of time horse-riding. There used to be a lot of filming going on around there and sometimes we'd get caught up in it. They'd be cyborgs walking down the street and bank robberies happening around us. Instead of washing cars for money, we used to go to the airfield and wash aeroplanes.

I've always had a liking for alcohol, ever since I was young. It made it easier for me to mix with people. And it just kind of carried on. I started working in a well-known up-market London store, did so for seven or eight years. I lived with friends on the edge of Richmond Park; we felt very lucky to be there.

Everything started to fall apart, though, around the time of the Green Park bombing. A bomb went off by my work and I started to go downhill. I did a geographical move, tried other jobs. They didn't work out. In the end, I moved cities altogether, still drinking like a fish.

I basically went on to drink myself out of jobs, out of money, ended up living in a squat. It was there that I met what I thought was a really nice bloke. We married, I became pregnant, the council gave us a flat. Unfortunately, he turned out to be a violent alcoholic. I had a son and daughter by him and he was violent towards my daughter. So that was the end of that.

His dad actually helped me get rid of him. I really, really, really wanted another child, so I basically went out and picked a bloke. My son doesn't know, and I've tried to find his dad, tried everything, but he literally vanished when he was two, completely vanished off the face of the earth.

I haven't touched a drop of alcohol now for eight years. I have six grandchildren and I love being a grandma; I just wish I had more energy. I end up doing art and crafts with them as I literally don't know how to play with children. For example, if they want me to go to a tea party with their dolls, I'm like, 'Er, OK...what do I need to do?!'

I've always been happy with my own company, watching TV and reading. I'm really into Jeffrey Archer at the moment and I love a good Catherine Cookson. I used to work in a second-hand bookshop between jobs; it was absolute heaven!

The best thing I ever did was get my diagnosis. Because now I know who I am and why I am. It answers so many questions, it gives me peace of mind. I really love myself now. Future-wise, what I really want to do is get my heart sorted out. Then I can get out and about more, have another dog, go riding again. There's a fairy festival I want to go to (I'm always away with the fairies). It's one where everyone dresses up, the trees included. There's tarot readings and folk music, lots of mindfulness. It's a magical atmosphere. Also, my brother lives down in Devon and so I want to go down to see him. The train journey goes along a stretch of track that keeps collapsing; the sea is on one side, the moor on the other. I really love that train journey.

Celeste

Word-lover

It was on a high-school field trip that a classmate suggested we share what items we'd want if stranded on a deserted island. I knew immediately. 'A dictionary,' I said. 'That way I would never be bored.' Everyone burst out laughing and I melted under the humiliation. I didn't understand why they found it so funny. The unexpected shame and the consequent mocking stayed with me for decades. It wasn't until I learned that my grandfather had read the dictionary cover to cover that my heart began to heal.

Midway through my 50s, my sister mentioned the word Asperger's to me. This began a period of intense study and soul searching that eventually opened my eyes. At last I understood the dictionary incident and the thousand others that had followed.

I'm a freelance writer, so my time is spent alternating between procrastinating and writing, procrastinating and doing housework, procrastinating and preparing meals. Watercolor painting and the internet are also sprinkled in between.

My favorite part of the day is my quiet time. I open my Bible, my journal and other books, and begin pouring over whatever topic hits my fancy that day. Heaven? Grace? Mercy? Peace? I dig deep into the Scriptures for life-giving strength. My husband will come in to kiss me goodbye and then I return to my topic. On a good day I can joyfully study the Word of God uninterrupted for three hours or more. My dictionary is always nearby.

The weakest area of my life is executive functioning. I struggle to have productive days because my brain is so dreadfully scattered. I'm so embarrassed at the randomness of it all. I often feel like a failure because of all the uncompleted writing projects piling up.

Late in the evening my husband and I pray together and kiss goodnight. He stays up afterwards while I go through my nightly rituals and head to bed, putting on lip gloss and hand lotion while I lie on my right side. I then immerse myself in complete darkness, flip over on to my left side and rest my head on the tiny pillow I've made by cutting up memory foam to the perfect size. Sleep comes quickly.

I used to be worried that someone would find out there was something wrong with me and take my children away. Now that my children are successful adults with their own kids, I battle the thought that I'm a lousy grandmother. I'm not like others who have grandchildren. Why can't I be normal?

After learning about Asperger's, all the pieces of the puzzle suddenly slotted in together. At last, I felt like I finally fitted in somewhere. Then I found out the 'experts' who write the DSM-5 had eliminated the diagnosis of Asperger's. Once again, I felt like a nobody. Over time, though, I came to understand their decision. They did the right thing. Asperger's doesn't belong in the *Diagnostic and Statistical Manual of Mental Disorders*. Asperger's isn't a mental illness. We simply have our brains wired differently!

I have a diagnosis for sure; I diagnosed myself. If I went to a psychologist or some other 'expert' for testing and they failed to officially diagnose me, it wouldn't change my own diagnosis. I would ask them, 'And how long have you been working with adults with Asperger's? How many years have you spent diagnosing Aspies? Well, let me tell you, I've had more than five decades of experiencing Asperger's first-hand. When you've had 50 years of experience, you come see me; and I'll give you another chance to get it right.'

Shortly after self-diagnosis I withdrew and turned even more inward than usual. I'd always held on to the wishful thinking that I would someday figure out how to become like everyone else. Suddenly, I realized I'd never be able to enjoy a lot of what others enjoy, like malls and concerts and public gatherings. I'd never be able to walk into a room and navigate the oceans of conversation. I'd never be able to do two things at once. I realized that I'd be doomed to have meltdowns for the rest of my life. Having a physical injury that laid me up for quite a while contributed to me almost becoming a recluse.

The few people I shared my revelation with let me know pretty quickly that it was better to keep my mouth shut. Living in a rural area added to the isolation, despite my family's total acceptance and support. Thankfully, I've been blessed with a wonderful, helpful husband. He's found the diagnosis very useful. In fact, he's greatly relieved to finally understand where I'm coming from, to truly accept that I've never purposely tried to make life hard for myself. I know that God would take care of me if something happened to him, but I don't like to think of what it would be like to face this world alone, to not have his understanding and cushioning in my life.

Now several years down the road from diagnosis, I feel like

I'm getting the old me back. I am grateful for the diagnosis, because it makes my life easier. I can cut myself some slack, and life has become more enjoyable. I understand why I have such an inordinately deep love and fascination for the Bible.

Studying the Bible in my own little corner in my own little room makes me happy. I love to dig into the depths of both the New and Old Testaments, searching out patterns and linking thoughts that aren't so obvious to others. I've written hundreds of Bible studies that I've shared with others over the years. I must admit, though, I've gotten into a bit of trouble with pastors in the past who've taken offense at my six-page-long letters questioning something they casually mentioned in their Sunday sermon. I wasn't saying they were wrong; I was just trying to learn more, to understand more. Now that my pastor is my own husband, we have hours and hours of Bible discussions. This gives me great joy.

I've had a good life, including a loving family growing up (although I didn't 'feel' that love at the time). I have a faithful husband and great kids; I've made numerous accomplishments throughout the years. Yet, before my diagnosis, every single year of my life I wished that I was dead. I couldn't understand why anyone would actually want to keep on living when they could go to heaven instead. But it's not as if I wished I was dead every day. It was just my default setting whenever I faced any problems.

One of my earliest memories is of lying on the floor in my closet among a heap of clothes, saying, 'No one loves me except God.' He has always been the One who has given me the strength to survive. At times I've even been able to thrive. I couldn't do any of it without the Holy Spirit; he is like my 24/7 mentor.

If you were to ask, 'What's the best thing about being me?' I'd have to answer, 'Nothing.' It brings tears to my eyes and a pain to my throat, but nothing's the best about being me. My family loves me, though; maybe that will do. And God. God will always love me.

Julie

Overthinker

I have an attraction to ginger hair. It doesn't seem to matter whether it's on a man or a woman. Most of my contemporaries now are either silver-haired or bald, though. So it's more a question of being attracted to a personality.

Appearance-wise, I usually wear colourful clothes. I've noticed that others in their 60s are starting to slip into 'old-age beige'. I've told my daughter to shoot me if I ever do that.

There was a time after my daughter left home when I was desperate to fill the gap. I've been in love now several times, both online and offline, but the feelings have only been reciprocated for a short time, if at all. It's as if I seem all right at first and then when they get to know me offline, they go off me. I'm not very good at sustaining the relationship. I don't know if this has been because of any Aspie behaviour, or my wariness because of my past. Maybe I just pick crap men! Or maybe it's because I like my time to myself, so I'm not there to prop up someone else's ego. I'm not a girly-girl and I don't like cooking, so that certainly doesn't help, as a lot of men in my age group rather expect you to look after them. Well, I had

25 years of doing literally everything for my ex, and I'm not doing that again.

I haven't done much online dating for a while now. I'm not saying I never will again, but I did get a bit jaded with it all. It was great at first, much easier than meeting someone in a bar. Unfortunately, you do have to meet them face to face in the end, and I'm not good at eye contact or flirting – all the stuff that's usually expected. On the plus side of Aspieness, I'm not good at lying either, so some men were amazed that I really did look like my photo!

I suppose I need to have a post-self-diagnosis relationship, see if it helps explain some of my oddities. Things like having a panic attack in a supermarket because of the fluorescent lights. Before I couldn't explain it, but now I know that sunglasses stop that happening. Hey, sunglasses all year round – they would get to go out with me looking like an ageing rock star! You never know, someone might be up for it...

I live alone right now. I have done for over 20 years, although always with a cat for company. A few hundred years ago I think I would have been burned as a witch. I wonder how many of those poor women were on the autistic spectrum, how many were considered too odd for their time.

I have a couple of friends I occasionally have lunch with, and I'm in a cribbage group and play matches in a league once a week. I'm very good at sustaining long and loyal friendships. Very different to acquaintances and their small talk. I think one of the joys of being retired is no one is going to sack or reprimand me for being rude (in their opinion). I no longer have to feign interest in things I couldn't care less about.

Another joy of retirement is being able to wake up naturally, no alarm clock. I start each day with half an hour of exercise: 15 minutes of yoga to stay supple, 15 minutes of running for my heart. I don't have the courage to run outside because whenever I have done, I've been laughed at. Apparently, I run funny. The running therefore is in a figure of eight around my lounge where no one can see me.

After breakfast and house chores, I'm back to the computer for my 'work'. I'm determined to keep my brain active as well as my body. I'm learning a language online, and I'm currently writing a book. I've always wanted to write but was so exhausted all my working life that I never managed it. I'm about three-quarters of the way through now, so I hope to finish it in the next few months. It might not come to anything, but that's OK. I just need to do it.

After some fruit and a bit of fresh air, I make a cuppa and read for a while. Or sometimes just sit down and think. I think a lot. I have an old black-and-white photo of me as a child, sitting head in hands, staring, not smiling for the camera like the other children. My mother said this was a frequent pose, and when she asked what I was doing, I'd just say, 'Thinking.' She found this very odd for a child, but it seems to be the essence of me. I wish I could remember what I was thinking back then.

Nowadays, I tend to overthink things a lot – the state of the nation, for example. I also spend more time worrying. If someone is five minutes late, I'll assume that they're dead in a ditch. I'm currently worried about terrorism, and also the effects of Brexit; I'm glad I don't have grandchildren who may suffer. I care and despair for the future, despite not having a personal stake in it. It'd be nice to leave the world in a better place than when I entered, but I think that's unlikely to happen.

If the weather is good, I like reading in my patio garden. It's only small but I'm proud it's the prettiest in the street. Pottering about in it – literally, as it's all pots – is one of the pleasures of my life. I also like watching detective stories in the evenings, especially *Sherlock* and *Vera, Endeavour, Lewis* and *Morse.* I've watched them all several times and feel a particular affinity to Morse. He lives alone with his opera and crosswords. And although he occasionally tries to have a relationship, they always go wrong, like mine.

I go to bed in the early hours, but I don't like going alone. I miss sex and wish I had someone to cuddle up to, especially when it's cold. Conversely, I'm glad to wake up alone and have the day to myself. So I've always got half of what I want...

I used to be married. He was my first serious boyfriend. Back then, we did it so young. I knew it was a mistake almost immediately, spent the next 25 years being manipulated and controlled. I was in low-paid jobs before any mention of equal pay; my income was miniscule. It meant I couldn't leave as I couldn't afford to go anywhere else. My parents wouldn't have me back as he didn't hit me, and psychological/social/emotional/financial control was not a consideration then. I couldn't even explain it to other people. He seemed so nice, so smart, a good earner; everyone thought I was lucky – why would I want to leave? And yet I did, because he wasn't so nice at home. I couldn't work out how to leave except by becoming a live-in servant and I didn't want to do that. It was how he treated me that I didn't like. He altered the way I looked. I wasn't allowed to wear make-up or have my hair short; he made me wear clothes that were frumpy. In photos of the married me, I am unrecognisable; the real me is absent. He repeatedly told me I was stupid and couldn't possibly do this or understand that. He even changed my name because he didn't like it. I won't go into further details because there are too many little things to list, and while each one is small, it's the accumulation of undermining and put-downs which kills you inside. Like a snowball getting bigger and bigger and eventually flattening you. After a while I couldn't leave because I had zero confidence in myself and was a nervous wreck. I developed eczema and my daughter gained a stammer. When he left, they both miraculously disappeared. I think that says it all.

When the divorce from my husband came through, I moved from the big family home to a little terraced house. With the leftover money, I bought a reasonable second-hand car from a garage recommended to me by another newly divorced female friend. The garage owner was such a lovely man that I took the car back there for servicing too.

One day, though, on my way to work the cam belt broke. Somehow, I managed to get out of the fast lane with no power or proper control. The AA was called, and they said the car was in a dreadful condition and hadn't been serviced. When I said I had it serviced regularly, he advised me to take it to another garage. I did so and was informed that the car had previously been a write-off, had been clocked and indeed had not been serviced. They said it shouldn't have been on the road and that I was lucky to be alive!

Then started the battle to get my money back. I didn't have any spare cash to go and buy another car and I couldn't afford a solicitor, so I went to Citizens Advice. I was told I had little hope of recompense. That's when my intense sense of justice and stubbornness kicked in. I needed the money, but I couldn't afford a solicitor. Instead, I devoted a year of my life to becoming familiar with the Sale of Goods Act. There was no easy internet access back then, so I spent all my spare time in the library studying books on law. When we got to court, it was the garage's solicitor against me. The solicitor was unprepared – he expected a walkover – whereas I could (and did) quote every clause and sub-clause of the Sale of Goods Act relevant to my case. The judge ruled I should get a refund and at long last I got justice.

I've never really talked about it since because I was ashamed to have got myself into that situation in the first place. But con men can only work because they're so plausible...and, years later I met his solicitor again through a work placement. I was surprised he remembered me, but he said he couldn't forget me as I was the only person who had ever got money out of him!

When I look back at my dad's family, I can see now the autistic black-and-white thinking. I was brought up by what would now be called a militant atheist and I was taken out of school assemblies and religious education. My father wouldn't do that if I was young now because religious education has changed and covers many faiths. In those days, though, it didn't, and he didn't want me indoctrinated in one faith. Instead, as he had travelled widely, and had the help of an encyclopaedia, he taught me himself all about each religion.

Even as a child, I was aware that my family was slightly different. Other people's families called themselves C of E (Church of England) and went to church for weddings, funerals, baptisms, maybe Christmas and Easter, but hardly seemed to think about their god much in between. I thought it odd then that they didn't really believe or care like our family did. Now I realise we were the odd ones; no one sat on the fence in our fervently divided family. Half were staunch atheists, the other half were in church every week, tithed, and produced missionaries (my cousins) who went off to Africa to spread the word. I don't know how this division came about. I would love to ask how and why this family became so opposed over religion, but anyone who might have known is now dead.

I'm an atheist myself. A strict atheist, I always say, which makes people laugh, but I mean it. I wouldn't dream of getting married in a church or having a child christened for social reasons. My daughter is gay, and one day I was saying to someone it was as well she was born to me because I love her unconditionally, whereas as a Catholic she might have found that a problem. I was consequently assured there was nothing in the Bible against homosexuality. I quoted Leviticus to her, and she had never even heard of Leviticus. I had to explain it was a book of the Bible to a confirmed Christian! That's the sort of thing I can't understand. Because I'm passionate about things, and don't know how you can call yourself a Catholic without knowing what you're expected to believe. She couldn't understand why I, as an atheist, would even want to know anything about the Bible or Qur'an, etcetera. But I don't do blind faith. And I don't do blind lack of faith either.

I have a couple of religious friends. We agree to disagree, but I could never have a relationship with anyone religious because to me believing in a god is like believing in fairies or Father Christmas. I couldn't respect that person in the way you should respect a partner. If a god ever makes an appearance, I am willing to change my mind, but meanwhile I find religions, and the psychology of their followers, absolutely fascinating in a strange way. The internet has probably turned my fascination into an obsession. It's all so accessible. I love watching discussions and debates between theists and atheists, but sometimes it's not so good for my blood pressure. After all these years, I'm still passionate about the subject and prone to shouting at the screen!

I'd like to live in a world without war. A world where all minorities would be respected and treated as equal, where people on all sorts of spectrums would be accepted and nurtured. It would all be very John Lennon's 'Imagine'. In reality, I realise that human nature will always find something to fight over.

I don't have an official diagnosis. I'd never even heard of Asperger's until I became a mother and started wondering why my child was a bit different. Even then I didn't associate it with me and the struggles I'd had. I think as I got older, though, I became less worried about what people thought about me. I let the mask slip. I can now see the connection between my late father, who was an out-patient at a mental hospital in the 1960s, myself and my daughter. By the time I realised I had ASD, there seemed no point in getting an official diagnosis.

Looking back, I wish I'd known earlier. I was always trying to fit in and not doing so, whereas my daughter has gone with her own flow and is doing very well. I remember coming home from work utterly exhausted, sitting at the table crying. It wasn't that I couldn't do the work; in fact, it was often too easy for me. What I couldn't understand was why I hated it all so much. I now realise things like the fluorescent lights and the noise of typewriters were all too much for me. My husband told me I was stupid, which didn't help. I would leave a job and go to another one, thinking it would be different. Of course, it wasn't. I had a lot of jobs, and consequently no progression. Towards the end of my working life I happened to be in small offices, much better for me environmentally. The people, though, I found very hard work. I think they felt the same about me! At one place I was never invited to the Christmas lunch for the full six years I worked there; I was left to man the phones instead. I know I wouldn't have been the life and soul of the party, but I would have made an effort.

I've been depressed on and off all my life, but I've chosen not to take my GP up on the offer of medication. I don't like the idea of chemicals altering my brain. I've phoned the Samaritans when close to suicide and I've talked to therapists in the past too. I now think that the depression may be associated with my Asperger's and so there's nothing to be done anyway. It's just part of me and I've learnt over the years how to accept and ride with it. It comes and, a day, a week, a month later, it goes. Until the next time. Exercising and eating the right foods has kept my body well; most people think I am at least ten years younger than I am. It's as if my body and my brain are quite separate and duel it out occasionally. Sometimes people who don't know me well tell me I am so lucky to be this healthy at my age. I am not lucky; I work at it. The unhealthy, unhappy part of me is invisible.

I speak to Julie again a few months later. She tells me that she's found the post-self-diagnosis relationship she'd been looking for 'with a lovely man I met at cribbage'. She informs me that, yes, as expected, being able to explain why she does some things which may seem odd has helped. Having him understand means that 'he cuts me extra slack'. She ends our contact summing up their relationship as 'so far, so good!' and I wish her all the best.

Christophe
Optimist

I talk to Christophe from the comfort of his own home. He's sitting in the lounge in an armchair by the window. The place is airy and light: 'Autistic people don't like dark colours.' He's dressed casually and quickly points out that that's not always the case. 'I like to dress spick and span when I'm going about my business. If I were to go out for a dinner, for example, then I'd dress the part. Shiny shoes and everything.'

He notices me looking up at the landscapes on the walls and points to the one above him. 'Can you see my picture? I do a bit of painting, watercolour and acrylic. I'm self-taught. It's similar to that one over there.' He points at another landscape hung up on the adjoining wall before briefly mentioning his famous artistic ancestry. 'I think that's where I get it from. Flashes of inspiration; of curves and shapes. Last year I made some artwork for a local charity. Even ended up joining a group and recording a song for them. We had the time of our lives together!'

I'm one of seven children, born in Yemen, in a bungalow-type building without a roof or a door. My birth coincided with the Suez Crisis when the West was trying to regain control of the canal. My father was in the Royal Air Force and I was guarded by a Gurkha.

I came to England at three months old, quickly contracted measles and became quite deaf. No one realised till I was nine. They just thought I was an idiot. From the age of nine till 15 I was made to speak with a speech therapist. So now I can speak 'like what they do down south'! I'm registered deaf, but I use BSL (British Sign Language). I also speak English and understand Arabic, French and German.

I live in a flat, a typical male hideaway in the suburbs. The centre of town is only five minutes away on my mobility scooter. I don't speak to many people when I'm out. They have their own worries that I don't need to know about; I'm just trying to get on through my day.

I live by myself but I'm married. When my wife was diagnosed with cancer, I said to her, 'I think it's best if you go live with your mother, your twin sister, your grandmother, your aunt and our son. They'll be able to look after you.' That then caused my marriage to break up. I thought I was being selfless. But my wife thought I was being selfish. Because she thought I should be looking after her. She thought I was rejecting her.

I'm still in touch with my wife, though. We're quite amicable. She's within a ten-mile journey from me. It can be done within 20 minutes because of the standard of the roads up here.

My son's autistic too. But on the other end of the spectrum. He's a 15-year-old friendly giant. I'm expecting him to pan out at 6 foot 2. He's very strong and he's shy. Whereas I am overfriendly. When we lived together, I found it very hard. I'd have to go into another room for fear of putting him down in such a way that he couldn't understand. Because he would be repeating sentences which would do my head in. I used to have to stand up and say, 'Right. It's time out for Daddy now.'

My wife copes with our son quite well. And he has the whole family around him now too; they all live together. The cancer is stage four, so if my wife dies, my sister-in-law will adopt him. They're like two peas in a pod anyway. It would be an easy transition for him. And I will still be around.

Job-wise, I'm actually a chef by trade. I used to run a three-star hotel in England and then I joined the Royal Air Force as a caterer. I was doing really well until nine months in when I was badly beaten up. Apparently, I didn't fit in; I didn't know why. I left catering and never returned. I moved into supermarkets but became bored after two years, and became a postman instead. It allowed me to work with people but on my own. I then met a wonderful girl, but we broke up abruptly and I tried to take my own life. I then began near enough stalking her; it took me two years to manage to stop. Ten years later I tried to take my own life again. I'm currently on antidepressants. Together with the autism, they leave me feeling pretty isolated.

I'm also retired now, but only because of my physical disabilities. My day-to-day life is dictated by painkillers. There's so many that need to be taken at different times and they all kick in at different intervals. A juggling act. I have different pressure points on my body as well. They dictate where and when I sleep. I don't travel too far as it's too stressful, as is too much contact with other people in general. Even though I'm deaf, I can feel the noise; it's just like I'm inside a dance club. I spend a lot of time at home therefore, enjoying my creative pursuits. I also love looking into my genealogy. I've gone all the way back to 1500.

I got my diagnosis just four years ago. It means I'm now an official card holder; it's my get-out-of-jail-free card. It shows the emergency services that I'm autistic and it's very useful as I have a big mouth! I try to be gracious, but I tend to speak my mind. I can be loving and kind, but I can also be crushingly hurtful.

Unfortunately, I think there's too much pressure on too few resources nowadays. Too many people need help. The professional services aren't really there anymore, not unless you can pay for them. I rely on my Polish friends upstairs. And my next-door neighbours. My disabilities mean that I've now been banned from driving, but sometimes my wife's family take me out to the supermarket in the car. I can't walk too far without my wheelchair, so my son pushes me round in it.

I still love my wife, so I don't go running after other ladies. I believe my wife is my best friend, etc, etc. She's my life.

I ask him how they met.

It was at my place of worship. I looked at her and I thought, as men do. She just grew on me. I started changing the way I was living, stopped the drinking, started saving. Because I knew I was going to marry the girl. Anyway, I saved like mad, got a little Fiat 126, which she adored. I thought she'd want a better car, but no, she loved it. We bought a house and everything.

Then, after three or four years, my son appeared on the

scene. Not long after, I started getting ill with angina and arthritis, fibromyalgia and asthma. We drifted apart when he was four. Got back together when he was nine. And now we're apart once more.

I ask if he thinks they'll get back together again. He pauses for a moment before answering.

No. Not now. Not now.

Clara

Superwoman

I miss my old neighbour a great deal. In summer, I used to go over to her with a tray of coffee and homemade cinnamon rolls. After she reached her 90s, she was more easily convinced to join in. We'd sit in the sun doing crosswords or I'd have her tell me something from when she was younger. I've lived here a decade and now know more about this area than those who've lived here for 40 years. That neighbour passed away a few years ago and I don't get along very well with the new one. Or most of them actually. They don't look at living 'together' the way I do. The garbage container is filled with stuff that should be elsewhere; it's full after one week and it's only emptied once a fortnight. They don't clean the common areas after use and they park their cars as they wish without paying for it. These things annoy me, and I have difficulty letting them go.

I'm a Swedish heterosexual Protestant. I'm 172cm tall and I'm a little bit overweight with naturally grey, short hair and glasses.

I struggle with waking up in the morning. But I do so every day at six. Once washed and dressed, I greet my dogs to a new day, give them a belly rub and a kiss. The curtains are pulled back and I check the weather and the thermometer. The leftover water in the kettle is poured into a jug to be used in my CPAP (continuous positive airway pressure machine) – a device that helps me cease snoring. I do the dogs' rations, then prepare my own. I take milk in my tea and real butter and cheese with my sandwiches.

After a short walk with the dogs, I'm off to a workplace where I train to get ready for real work after a long period of sick leave. Back at home, I take a quick bite for lunch and then we go out again, this time for a longer walk.

We live in a small village and don't have a lot of roads for our walks. We have a nice little forest instead. On the outskirts there are farms with cows and horses. The village itself consists of houses dating back a couple of centuries as well as those built only last year. I live very close to the church whose roots go back to at least the 14th century. I rent a one-bedroom flat in a ground-level house and have a front yard and a back garden. I try to change the greens and flowers for berry-bearing bushes that don't need a lot of care. I have black fingers you see, not green.

My ASD was diagnosed in my early 60s. Many people have asked why, after living a full life undiagnosed, it matters now. They are right: I have lived a full life. But I have done so by copying others. It's made it possible to work, achieve things, experience a lot of fun, etc. But I've always been a wreck at home. I've never been able to invite someone over for coffee spontaneously, for example; I've always ended up exhausted from cleaning the house beforehand. I was never able to understand why; it was like I was two different people. It's a relief now to receive help in the home twice a week.

I like to think of myself as one who thinks outside of the box. I've had different jobs and many hobbies. I tend to learn all I can about what I'm into, so I consider myself a bit of a superwoman. That was an epithet I got from someone else some 30 years ago, but it stuck. I've a very good long-term memory and what I've learnt is always still there. I'm an optimistic person and I've said that once I get this help to sort my house, I'll not need help in the future. I'm now beginning to realise that I'll need help for the rest of my life. That thought, though, isn't depressing or scary.

Sometimes I miss having a sex partner but, when considering the options, I believe I'm better off without. I currently sing in a choir and I also attend a gym health class. I'm not good at chit-chat, so I time my arrival for when we're about to start, make sure that I leave as soon as we're done.

For some reason, I can neglect the fact that I need to go to bed. Especially if the next day is a work one; I often end up going out very late with the dogs. We've met the badger a few times, but he's not very friendly; he turns his back on us. Sometimes we hear the call of the cuckoo or smell the scent of the fox. In wintertime, we often see footprints of hare and deer while the nightingale sings in a tree nearby; so lovely to hear in those late hours.

Hannah

Creator

My biggest concern with ASD is the isolation, now and in the future. I'm very self-contained, so it's an isolation of my own making. I'm retired, and while I'm quite happy with my own company, I'm realizing more and more that I need others in my life.

The one thing that keeps me from living completely in my own head is the presence of my two dogs. They were both rescued from abusive situations; they both have their own special needs that must be seen to. I'm constantly thinking about those needs, constantly making sure they're being met. I've always had an affinity with animals, especially dogs. I can look at them and be able to tell exactly what they're thinking: silent communication. It's a skill that I'm totally lacking when it comes to my own species. It's the main reason why isolation is an issue; I tend to avoid social situations that I needn't attend. When I'm with neurotypical people, I focus on being present in the moment, not in my head. I pay close attention to what's being said; I'm constantly weighing up whether I have anything relevant to add. It's exhausting maintaining that level of focus just to spend time with and be accepted by people who don't know I'm on the spectrum. I'm not ashamed of my autism, but not everyone has a clear understanding of what it is and how it affects the individual. I disclose my diagnosis only when I feel it's safe to do so. I never tell casual acquaintances as they might tell everyone else and it might change the relationships I've built.

I feel it's valuable for me to have time with other people. I love to laugh and it's much more fun to do it with others. I volunteer weekly at an intercity church to help fund their community outreach programs. I've found everyone there to be very accepting, but I have to work hard to be 'normal'. I like the feeling of giving back and helping others, the sense of contribution. The hard work is therefore worth it. I think I'm perceived as very earnest, hardworking and committed. I thought I was doing a really good job of projecting normal, but just this week one of the church members said to me, 'You're always working. Work, work, work. You never stop work and just sit down and chat with us.' Aha, someone or everyone *has* noticed that I'm different... Do they think I'm shy? Stuck-up? At the end of the day, we all want to be accepted; I'm no different. They've always expressed their gratitude for my hard work, but now I'm questioning the acceptance I thought I had. It was probably just a casual observation with no real meaning behind it, but whenever something like this catches my attention, I have the tendency to roll it around in my mind, worrying away until I come to terms with it. I wish I didn't do this, but it seems to be my process to make sure I didn't miss an important message.

I enjoy having friends, but until recently I was undercutting these friendships by not being able to maintain them.

The adage 'to have a friend you have to be a friend' has always been my undoing. I've only recently realized that if a friend calls to chat about day-to-day nothings, fulfilling their need for this is an important part of being a friend. And meeting for a meal in a noisy, echoing restaurant, which sets my nerves jangling, that's also part of being a friend. And so's going shopping at the mall together (No! Not that!). That aspect of friendship – the constant exchange of small talk and the minutiae of life – was just beyond my comprehension. It was everything I didn't understand the need for, and so friends drifted away without me even noticing until they were gone. I have, though, managed to retain five close friends. They all date back to my teens and early 20s. Tellingly, they all live hundreds or thousands of miles away from me. We talk/text/Skype/email frequently, but it's all devoid of that small-talk element. Perhaps it is that very distance that allows me to feel so close to these people. They don't make demands on my daily life. When I see one of them – which can be anywhere from once a year to once every five years – we pick right up where we left off; that bond of friendship is still so strong. I enjoy every second spent together yet can't help but wonder if it would be the same if we lived in the same town. Would my inability to do friendship maintenance change things? Whatever the case, I cherish my close friends who've accepted that I'm slightly different, yet still a fun person to be around.

I grew up in the 1950s, a time when people weren't yet familiar with the term 'autism'. I suspect that my father was on the spectrum. He was remote and rigid, with a list of rules that must be adhered to, no matter what the circumstances. I can only remember two moments of connection with him that weren't about me doing something wrong. My mother was extremely socially aspirational. She viewed my brother and me as the means to raise her social status; she expected us to accomplish great things. As my brother is a classic male Aspie (not diagnosed) with dyslexia and I am an Aspie with ADHD, we were totally unsuited to fulfill the roles my mother had assigned to us. This led to my brother and me being constantly berated for being so stubborn or uncooperative, for not doing as she wished. She was unable to see that neither of us had the skills to do as she required. Apart from their false expectations, we were pretty much ignored by our parents. I learned at a very early age the value of self-reliance; I was definitely on my own.

While my brother struggled in school, I was labeled as 'gifted'. This didn't help my mother's expectations. When I started kindergarten, I was very self-contained; it was the first time I'd been surrounded by so many other children. I repeatedly heard that I needed to 'try harder' to be a part of the group (I've since heard this phrase countless times). There were 20 of us in my class, including another child whom I now recognize as being Aspie. A classic 'Little Professor' who was obsessed with furnaces and all things mechanical. It's always struck me that out of the 20 in a typical middle-class suburb, 10% of us were on the spectrum. I firmly believe that figure reflects the true percentage of Aspies in the population. There must be so many undiagnosed individuals out there. In the same class we also had a little boy, Bertie, who had microcephaly. He was my favorite playmate – the perfect companion for a little girl who found her peers bewildering. At home I was punished for flapping my hands, but at recess Bertie and I would happily sit together, flapping our hands and laughing. We both enjoyed it hugely; we didn't need words. When my teacher complimented my mother on her daughter's compassion for playing with Bertie (whom all the other children ignored), my mother was incensed that I would rather play with 'the dummy' than make friends with more socially acceptable children. That was the beginning of the war between my mother and me.

It lasted until her death. She refused to accept my true self and constantly forced me into situations where I was unable to cope. Meltdowns were common, and she couldn't accept that I found so much around me completely overwhelming. Food, noises, smells, textures, etc.

Throughout school, I was always being called to the principal's office where they would confront me with the comparison between my high standardized test scores and my mediocre class grades. They'd demand to know the reasons behind the differences; they'd demand an explanation for my lack of involvement with other students, my lack of involvement in school activities in general. It was an acknowledged fact that I was an outsider and an underperformer. No one knew what to do about it, though, so, time and time again, I was merely urged to 'try harder'. What no one could grasp was that I was trying as hard as I could, that I was adrift in a world that I found increasingly baffling.

Work was just a series of mundane jobs until I returned to college to study graphic design. I became a typesetter and then a graphic designer. I'm a very visual person. I loved the process of producing the work and I got immediate satisfaction when seeing a finished piece in front of me. I was employed in art studios with other creative people, an ideal setting for me as I didn't stand out. I was surrounded by people expressing their individuality through their dress and personalities. I was inspired by eloquence and activism in other people; I still am today.

I married late, but as a very independent person, I found marriage difficult. I quickly realized I'd made a huge mistake, but I tried to make it work. I'd known my husband for 11 years prior to marriage, and he was very accepting of my quirks. We parted amicably after 12 years of marriage and he is still a good friend to me. I often wonder if my decision to marry was about doing something socially acceptable, rather than being what I really wanted to be. I never wanted children, perhaps because my parents made my own childhood so unpleasant. In retrospect, I realize that those early years were filled with rather a lot of emotional abuse.

While I've always known I was different to everyone else, I've never seen myself as flawed. A friend described me once as 'laid-back but intense' and I think that captures me perfectly. I'm easy-going, but I have a dedication to doing the best job I can do in all aspects of my life. I've accomplished things I'm proud of, I've been self-reliant, I've traveled extensively, I've had unique experiences. I took care of my mother in her later years with far more compassion than she ever gave me; I learned to forgive. My biggest accomplishment has been having a life well lived; I have very few regrets and it's far from over yet.

Later this year I'm moving 300 miles away to a place where I know no one. The move's driven by two factors: looking for a more temperate climate, and the fact that the only anchor that is really holding me here is the presence of my brother. Because of our dysfunctional upbringing, we aren't close. He's largely unaware of me and what goes on in my life. I've spent

40 unsuccessful years trying to build a relationship with him and his wife. I've come to loathe holidays and family events; spending time with the two of them always leaves me feeling dismissed and diminished. I'd rather check out of the family altogether than experience those feelings again.

I like to think that I have one more Big Adventure in me. I've worked out a strategy for getting to know new people. It revolves around lots of volunteering and getting involved at the local senior center; they've lots of classes there that look interesting. I've really blossomed since I was diagnosed, and I want to enjoy my new attitude, self-confidence and self-esteem in a new place, building a new life that's unhampered by work or family. It's a scary prospect but an exciting one too. I'll be 'working without a net' until I get established and build a few relationships. I've moments when I'm overwhelmed by the thought of the amount of effort this will take, but those moments are countered by my thoughts of excitement over a fresh start. I know it seems like the last thing an aging Aspie should do, but I need to do it while I still can. I'm trying hard to live my life with no regrets.

In preparation for the move, I'm now sorting through the accumulations of a lifetime, whittling my possessions down into 'keep', 'trash', 'donate'. Things have always been more important to me than people; I've acquired so many objects... Bookends with dogs on, plaques from the 1930s, old photos, distressed pieces of furniture. With my diagnosis came the realization that my acquisitive nature had much to do with the emptiness I'd felt my entire life. I knew that I was different, but I didn't know why. With my diagnosis, I feel like I've been freed from the need to fill the empty spots in my life with things. I'm letting them go and it feels good.

My diagnosis came just a few years ago; ASD level 1 (there are three levels that identify support needs; level 1 indicates the lowest need). As the diagnostician said, 'We used to say Asperger's.' That's how I identify: Asperger's. I'd suspected I was on the spectrum for about ten years before diagnosis. A friend's son had just been diagnosed and, out of curiosity, I started researching it. I immediately said, 'That's my brother, that's my dad', and finally, 'That's me!' Those undiagnosed but suspecting years were hard. I thought I finally knew what caused me to be who I was, but without a diagnosis I couldn't embrace it.

The journey to diagnosis was frustrating. I was unaware that not all therapists were knowledgable about the autism spectrum. I spent a lot of time, money and angst being dismissed because most of them had trained when Asperger's was still considered a male condition. More than one professional did more harm than good. I found that most clinicians – whom we need in order to be diagnosed – do us a grave disservice by not being aware of the huge group of undiagnosed people on the spectrum. They don't seem prepared to refer us to people who actually have the knowledge to recognize us. They want to diagnose us with something else instead. If you're a child, there is a wealth of informed clinicians, but the older you get, the fewer they become.

When I finally received my diagnosis, it was the best day of my life! So empowering, so freeing. I'd always been hard on myself, beating myself up over every misstep or faux pas. Frustrated, because I hadn't been given the Code of Universal Knowledge – my name for all the things that seem to occur naturally in the neurotypical population, but that are totally lacking in Aspies – all those social cues. The reasons why I heard things other people couldn't hear, why some touch hugely disturbed me, why people often got frustrated with me without me understanding why. The reasons why some smells irritated me so much while others had the opposite effect, why I had a strong aversion to certain colors and textures, why talking on the phone was so hard... With diagnosis, everything suddenly made sense. I could finally understand my behavior. I could choose to either modify it or avoid unnecessary situations altogether. I gave myself permission to make mistakes and I gave myself permission to learn from them.

I am now more content, happy and optimistic than I've ever been. I can even laugh at myself now! My one regret is that I had to wait so long to solve the mystery of me, to have that life-changing diagnosis. I wonder how different my life would have been if I'd been diagnosed earlier...

JoBo

Questioning Wanderer

I've been living in Northern California now for seven years and I have a girlfriend in the Philippines. We met via the internet. She's 60 and I'm 68 and we've been together a few years. She's also some kind of neurodiverse. She's got the most incredible memory. She can recall the most random moments in her past – time, date, day of week, clothing worn, activity, etc.

I'm currently planning my latest trip over to see her. We seem to be marrying when I get there. I've created a special digital spreadsheet on my smartphone for different levels of saving required for this excursion. It covers a full year. I realize that most people wouldn't do this, but since finding out about autism six years ago, I've come to notice that there are many differences between myself and the typical person. There always has been; I just didn't realize there was an explanation for it. Not until a Medicare psychologist suggested I look up 'Asperger's syndrome'. Since then it's been revelatory.

I've had relationships before, but they haven't lasted. They all ended because of unknown differences. I was married in my 20s for six years, but my wife ran away with our two-year-old child.

Apparently, this was due to my fascination with detailed axioms about life via an applied religious philosophy (I think subconsciously I wanted to fix something about myself). My wife would balk at my interests, while engaging in conversations with our apartment manager. It felt like she was making it clear that I was on the outside of her socializing abilities. It hurt, but I didn't understand why. Now, five decades later, I finally understand.

Because of the internet, it feels like my current girlfriend is right by my side, when in fact she's over 7000 miles away. She's dedicated to loving me, to understanding me. It's kind of a huge surprise as I've never experienced love like this before, not even from my mom or dad (perhaps they were too war-torn after WWII; they divorced in my teens). Sometimes I tell her that I hope my age-related chronic illnesses (cardio and diabetes) along with my Asperger's traits and the distance don't chew away at our relationship. She lets me know, though, that she has enough innocent positivity to move a mountain.

I'm only on social security so there's sometimes a conflict between mind and heart over whether I'm making the right decision. Am I being rational? Am I being practical? My mind thinks how extreme it is to be making even one or two international visits. My heart, meanwhile, says that I'm lucky to have found someone so late in life. It says, 'Stay with her, never leave her, your heart feels too much for her.' I know I would feel too alone without her, due in part to all the loneliness in my life so far.

The maintenance guy who helps with my mobile home turned around to me once and said, 'You don't know what you're doing.' He says I should just visit a prostitute instead. I found his address on Google maps, sent him a postcard to tell him

I know as much as anyone knows about getting into marriage. To me, it's absurd to follow social norms without question. Somehow, it seems more socially acceptable to visit a prostitute than get married to the one you love. Crazy!

Much of the communication with my girlfriend is carried out over the internet. I had an ex once who couldn't understand my preference for the internet versus the phone. We'd have rare phone chats, but I preferred texting. After we broke up, she got screaming mad at me for it. I told her that speaking on the phone would get me emotionally too close to her again, but I don't know if she really got it.

As a child, I had a deep but unknown curiosity for the flows of neurotypical conversation. My earliest memory is of teenage me rigging up a home kit intercom system between my room and my sister's next door. I'd listen in to the conversations she had with her friends when they visited. I wasn't trying to invade her privacy; I just wanted to understand. I think she could hear the click when I tuned in to listen, though, so it wasn't long before the jig was up.

There was another listening-in moment in my latter teenage years. It involved a friend. This friend had a younger sister who was blossoming, and I had an intense puppy-dog infatuation with her. I still wanted to get in on the neurotypical flows of conversation, to find out what people talked about and how. If I did this, it'd mean I'd have a better chance of getting to know her, of spending time with her. I rode a couple of miles to their house with great intent on my ten-speed bicycle. I hid below the side-wall kitchen window to try to listen in on any conversation. Unfortunately for me, it was a very quiet day inside; no new data for me.

Later in life, I had a Spanish girlfriend. I recall lecturing her during a road trip about how life is like a series of cubistic occurrences. Little did I know that my views were such because of being on the autistic spectrum. A psychologist later helped me understand that what I was referring to was in fact what the rest of the world referred to as flows of conversation.

Most of the time I'm OK being like a little fish in my little fishbowl, focusing on what I want, when I want. On rare occasions, though, it hurts when I look back at the vast ocean of life that I went through. A vast void sea of loneliness, occasionally feeling that there was no such thing as true friendship.

I feel a bit sad realizing I got through high school and college without any friends. I had friendly conversations, of course, but that was it; they'd be very brief and to the point. I don't really feel that friendship exists, though. People can say, 'I visited my friend', like it's some kind of absolute. But I don't think there are any absolutes in the physical universe, just what you think a friend to be. I have a heart for whoever I connect with, but the affinity doesn't get registered by most people. It's as if their antennae are only tuned into prospective friends with gift-of-the-gab flows. If that gift's not there, then their antennae are blunt towards you.

Those antennae were definitely blunt when I was at school. I therefore made my own entertainment. When other kids were playing with each other at break times, I was playing with my 8mm movie camera or the school studio TV camera. I loved the process of animation. I was fascinated by how manipulating one frame at a time could make the images come alive. I remember mastering the technique of sneakily looking through the school garbage bins for remnants of other kids' lunches.

It's how I saved enough lunch money from my dad for an 8mm camera I had my eye on. I found some pretty tasty sandwiches in those bins!

Later in life, my dad introduced me to electronics, an industry where details became something tangible. I was hooked. Unfortunately, I was sacked after 11 years due to my inability to interface well with others. After that, I took on small jobs like newspaper delivery and telemarketing, a variety of tasks to remain independent, to survive.

Looking back now, I wish people had been more understanding to me. I've experienced such meanness over the years and I've seen first-hand how being subjected to that cuts away at large segments of your life. I'm now medically retired, but I've still got an interest in technical projects. For the last two years I've been working on digital forex market analysis. It's unlikely to ever make me money, but it's something that I enjoy.

I speak to JoBo again a few months later. He's just come back from getting married in the Philippines. I see a photo of the two of them, huge smiles on their faces. He says about how hard the distance is now they're physically apart again. 'We love each other so much. Sometimes we break down as the miles between us can seem so ominous. I still feel so happy, though. Because at least I've managed to make one major human-to-human affinity connection, before I leave this world.'

Our 70s
and Beyond

Sanana

Scavenger of Facts

As a child, I remember stamping my feet when I felt angry, crying if I felt anything else. I still do the latter with any correction or disappointment. It does nothing for my self-esteem. I was raised in a very devout Catholic family. I was pretty much ignored by my mother. I was her eighth pregnancy, so I assume she was burned out by motherhood. My father and a few of my siblings made up for the deficit, though. I remember one sister, who was 15 years older than me, living at home till she married at 30. I recall waiting impatiently for her and my dad to come home from work for a little attention. She was a good sister; she even took me on dates with her if going somewhere she thought I'd be interested in.

I wish I'd known about Asperger's back then. As it was, I didn't find out till ten years ago, at 68. I've since been on a road of discovery. And I've encountered many surprises and challenges along the way! I've felt shock, identification, relief and excitement. Excitement for a long-sought-after answer to the last six decades of my life. After that I was angry. Angry at co-workers but also doctors and nurses that I worked along the side of, people that may have already known but never told me. I used to work in pediatric hospital nursing for many years, you see, but then I left it to do hospice work. If I'd stayed, maybe I'd have been exposed to the condition sooner...

I realize now that I had a few episodes of burnout during my career. I countered them by moving on to a new place. Looking back, I can see that it was when my co-workers were starting to see through my mask; I was treading on ever thin ice. Luckily, I never had a problem getting a new job. I had a state license and a good record. All in all, I had about 15–20 jobs over a 50-year period in several different states. Even one overseas as an employee of the Department of Army Civilians. The jobs that worked out best for me were the ones where I worked with just one other person, like a nurse's aide, so I was in charge.

Eventually, it actually was my work that led me to a diagnosis. I was in shift-report one evening when it was mentioned as a secondary diagnosis of a 13-year-old patient that had just been admitted. Because of my lack of knowledge of Asperger's, I had to ask how it was spelled and for a little background. As soon as my shift was finished, I proceeded to my bible, 'the big green book' (*Nelson's Pediatrics*). In it there were two large paragraphs of information which changed my life forever. I was excited; I felt this giant boulder lift from my shoulders. I realized that my brain is different, different in a not-so-bad way. I wasn't just an overly sensitive person with ADD (attention deficit disorder); there was an even bigger issue that I was born with. I could finally lighten up on myself, not take the blame for all my social and communication issues. I self-diagnosed, then eventually got the nod from two psychiatrists. They saw I was too old to go through an official assessment; they saw it wouldn't be of any benefit, as by then I was already retired.

I went on to spend a lot of time trying to learn as much as I could about Asperger's. I became quite obsessed, reading books and online references right through into the wee hours. It explained so many areas of my life; no wonder I was anxious and sometimes depressed. I've come to understand that repeated reliving of negative situations of the past (which I did for a few years) only leads to intense frustration, wasted time and emotions. I've found one good way to block rumination is to use the word 'STOP' whilst visualizing the traffic sign. It really helps me to regain thought control. Also, I started a practice of saying a devotional or motivational phrase to help me 'get out of myself'. It reminds me of my purpose in life: to help those newly diagnosed and to raise acceptance within communities.

Friendships have always been a bit of a mystery to me. I wish I hadn't spent so much of my precious time on trying to make them. I wish I'd been more of a friend to myself, but my self-esteem was always too low. Any overtures of friendship on my part were rejected, so I masked and copied others until I lost my own identity. If someone asked me any personal questions about my thoughts or opinions, I was at a complete loss.

It wasn't until fairly recently that I realized the importance of boundaries: that one should be taught how to form and express these boundaries, so people are less likely to take advantage. Knowing this and being able to act on it is of benefit to one's self-respect. Unfortunately, though, caution is still my first train of thought if someone tries to befriend me. That is, once I've got over the surprise and rule out any questionable motives.

Now the challenge for me in life is to release all the negativity of my past so that I can sow more love to others and myself. Forgiveness, insight and understanding have led to me finding my faith once again. Now, as a senior widow, I pursue personal prayer time, laughter and nature. I get comfort from my church family, a few friends and relations. I also have two fur babies – a Shih Tzu and a Maltipoo – who help to relieve my anxieties.

Paula
Retiree

I think the more support autistic adults can get the better. I've lived through over seven decades with a disability. Because of a lack of support, I either denied it or wished it were some other handicap.

I'm of average height and average build and my hair is light brown in color. I'm fairly slim and I've got a roundish face. My husband is of slender build and of average height for a man – i.e. he's taller than me.

About three years ago we sold our house and bought a condo unit in a small condominium building. There are 17 units altogether. Ours faces the back, so we see lots of trees and hear lots of birds, especially in spring. It's fairly close to downtown and there is a Dairy Queen nearby. Every Monday morning, the residents meet for coffee and food; we have a nice social time. I'm also involved with several other social activities outside the building. Sometimes, however, I get overwhelmed with it all and choose to 'stay home' instead.

One of the things I really like about living in this building is the homely smell of meals being cooked as I take my walk along the communal hall. It reminds me of all the happy times growing up with my family.

I was closest to my father (especially later on in my childhood). Then it was my elder sister, then my mother. Lastly, there was my younger sister. It was that sister whose interests were so different to mine. As a result, I found it really hard to get along with her. Later she said she'd always had trouble figuring me out. I wonder if that was the autism.

Before retiring, I was working in a factory that assembled small electrical parts. It was routine work; that's why I liked it. I'm proud to say that I lasted over 11 years there. It's because of that achievement that I now have a 'decent' retirement and I'm enjoying it. I'm learning every day about how to act 'normal', how to be genuine. I'm trying to focus on how other people feel when I interact with them, while at the same time making sure I don't overdo it. I like to tell jokes; it comes easier than just kidding around with jest and such like.

My ambitions now include being able to know that people are happy to have me in their life. I like to help people on social media, but I also like to spend time with people in real life. I sell beauty products freelance and I go to Bible study groups. I also make myself present at a regular Meetup group nearby.

I've never liked the idea of sexual relations. Before meeting my husband, I'd always thought the main purpose of sex was to produce children. I'd had lots of boyfriends, but either they liked me and I couldn't stand them or vice versa. Finally, though, I met someone who had also dated a rash of partners with a similar outcome. We met at a church camp; we were both in our early 30s. He seemed shy and unsure of himself and I thought I could help him. We had a church wedding and a lovely reception after.

I love my husband dearly, but unfortunately he's recently developed some health problems. This means he has trouble with his mouth making too much saliva. We both also sometimes snore, so we now sleep in separate rooms.

My husband and I have never had any sexual encounters with anyone other than each other. When we were in our 40s, though, we went through a bit of a bad patch. My husband started showing a lot of affection to a young girl half his age, and I started flirting with her father. It was her mother (his wife) who put a stop to it all (smart lady). Being on the spectrum made the whole situation much harder to deal with. It's an event that, looking back, really hurt me, but we got over it. We've been married now 38 years.

Harry

Realistic Autistic

I'm a 74-year-old autistic man living in Canada, a retired psychology teacher, short and bald. I was raised Jewish in a blue-collar family, the youngest and the only male offspring. The term 'autism' was unheard of when I was born.

I wasn't a happy child; I was labeled a 'cry-baby'. I wasn't very sociable, I preferred to play by myself. My stimming was physically punished at home and at school. As well as the 'cry-baby' label, I was also given the labels 'smart' and 'a bit strange'.

When I was 13, I rejected my home culture and became a full-blown juvenile delinquent. This allowed me to take on an identity I felt comfortable with: the Lone Wolf. This identity fitted in with my autistic view of the world. I survived by adapting to whatever social role I found appealing: truck driver, poet, warehouse worker, college student, professor, bookstore clerk, pool hustler. I became them all and many more in between.

I wasn't diagnosed till I was 70. It led to a very difficult period of adjustment that culminated in my having a large meltdown. I was subsequently arrested for assault. I then also lost my home. This resulted in having to deal with my autism directly, which in turn has brought me to a more balanced view of autism and my life. All of this could have been easier to deal with if there'd been some form of support for adult autistics. Unfortunately, that just doesn't exist around here.

I currently live in a fifth wheel out in the west. It's only in the last year that I've learned how to use self-care. My daily life now consists of routines, just like it does for so many autistics. Routines allow me to feel in control; they help me. I'm rehabilitating from spine and neck surgery, so I do a lot of walking each day. Building strength, re-learning how to move.

I have no close friends. I'm alone most of the time, but I'm comfortable with that. I like the silence. That doesn't mean I don't like music, though; I really do. I'm learning now to play the didgeridoo. I find the drone of this instrument so primal. It instantly calms me; it centers me.

I can see that I don't express empathy to other human beings, even though I feel it and can express it to animals. I know that I don't read people's facial expressions accurately. I know that I'm terrible when it comes to intimate relationships. I've been married six times, currently separated from my last wife. I'm good at seduction but bad at intimate communication and bonding. I learned seduction by copying other males. Everything else was disastrous.

I don't believe that my autism interferes with my daily life anymore. I have a blog which I hope helps older autistics feel more comfortable in themselves. I hope it helps them express their opinions about autism in their life, or whatever else they may want to express. I'm evolving to be an advocate for neurodiversity and a voice against ableism. I no longer think about the role of autism in my daily life in terms of how 'I pass.' I think instead of how 'I fit'.

Alice

Beach-girl

When I was a teenager, I had a pen-pal. Back then it was very common to have pen-pals. My mum had one from Finland and I had one from Vietnam. Mine was a gentle soul who worked as a flower vendor. I remember the civil war in Vietnam was just beginning when my pen-pal enlisted in the South Vietnamese Army. Things were just starting to explode over there. Footage of the war was shown on TV each night. Piles of dead bodies, bombed cities, villages burned, people on the run. Months and years passed by. I didn't hear from my pen-pal and I assumed he'd lost his life.

Last year I was fiddling with Google maps and for some reason ended up looking at his home city of Saigon. I remembered his address and typed it into the search bar. The map showed that his house still existed. So I wrote. I wanted to tell any surviving family or neighbour who remembered the boy that I did too. I wanted to tell them that I still have a scrapbook of the cards and photos that he sent all those years ago. Well, a couple of weeks later, a letter arrived at my house with Vietnamese stamps. It was from my pen-pal himself! He had survived the war, rebuilt the home as well as the flower business. He joked that today young people use the internet to converse around the globe, but in our youth it was aerograms! He was so happy to know that I'd not forgotten our correspondence. I think that as we age, there is always some nostalgia for our youth, and for times that seemed more innocent and more immediate than the present day.

I remember being a pretty good child at school. I never got into any trouble but that's probably because it was the 1950s; one simply didn't act up or misbehave. You spoke in class only if the teacher asked you a question. We still had dunce caps and the paddle. I was smart, so I got by OK. Everything changed when my hormones arrived. I couldn't handle the changes. I had a terrible year-long depression. Back then no one knew about Asperger's or the morbidity of depression.

Although I had my pen-pal for a while, I didn't have any actual friends in high school and I never went on a single date. No parties or dancing for me. No one ever asked me. I was smart, but I wasn't good-looking or funny.

College in the 1960s was better. I fitted in at a time when everyone wanted to be different. I had friends and a lover. I hitchhiked across the USA and Canada. Work, though, was a trial. Too boring. Too much stress. The only jobs I could do were menial ones like file clerk. Thank the gods this was before computers! I just had tons and tons of paper to manage. Life was still tough, though. I made bad relationship choices. I thought any man who wanted to get in my pants loved me. Idiot. I couldn't recognise the faces of co-workers if I saw them out of our work area. I couldn't drive because of stress, the speed, the noise. Barking dogs made me run in circles with hands over my ears. I couldn't bear the feel of cloth on my neck or chest, so I'd wear low-cut tops. I remember hearing co-workers talking behind my back about my choice of attire.

The stresses of day-to-day life meant that I couldn't even be present when my mum was dying. I took long walks instead. Subsequently, she died alone and I still hate myself for letting that happen. Over the years I've let so many people down because when times have got tough, I've just crumbled and run. Everyone thinks I'm a loser with a lousy character. I used to agree with them. I used to wonder what was wrong with me. And then, about ten years ago, I happened upon an article in the paper. Suddenly, things made sense. Asperger's. My nervousness, shyness, un-coordination, love of animals over people, and, most of all, my inability to function under stress.

I joined the Buddhist church a decade ago. It's helped me to calm my mind and stay centred. The church is one of the few public places where I feel at ease. I've tried different things over the years. I couldn't even jump rope as a kid but in my 30s I started taking dance classes. I got up to five hours a week. I'm pleased to say that my coordination did improve! I can toss paper at the bin now and it goes in! However, with aging comes a slow and steady unravelling of our coping skills. I joined a ladies' group here in our senior community, tried my hardest to fit in. But telling jokes and discussing food is not my kind of thing, so I dropped out after a year. Undeterred, I recently joined a group of ladies who knit and crochet at my senior centre. It's going OK, but I'm really not into grandchildren like they are. I sit by myself in case I say something that would offend them.

I feel that my diagnosis came too late in life. I was already in my 60s at the time. My hormones had already dictated my life for decades; they'd caused so many unpleasant consequences. If a man broke up with me, I'd fall into long depressions. When one is depressed, one makes poor decisions. After one particularly painful breakup, I quit my job and moved 400 miles away, just so I wouldn't have to see him again. By the time I'd heard of Asperger's, most of my relatives were already dead. Too many people had already been hurt and let down. I had already been left with too little in the way of financial resources.

Obsessions are part of daily life for someone with Asperger's and I still have them despite my age. For example, I currently have an obsession with Pomeranian dogs. I think to myself, 'I want a Pomeranian', but I know deep down I don't really want one. So I read books on Pomeranians, I look at breeders' websites for Pomeranians, I'm seriously tempted to get a Pomeranian. The sensation of wanting is so very powerful but I resist. I think, 'Thank goodness I can fight it off', but then, the next day, it's back, and I'm asking my partner, 'Can I get a Pomeranian?'

Pin

Philosopher

I was quite taken aback when my mother said, 'Is your daughter a drama queen like you were?' I never had a notion that I was overly dramatic, ever.

I was raised Catholic in a traditional Irish style. My mother, however, presented me with many Asian philosophical concepts and I evolved to Taoism – no particular sect, just a personal philosophy based upon Confucianism and the *Tao Te Ching*. She was bisexual, so I grew up with all sexual orientations and gender identities being acceptable. I'm gender-ambivalent with female parts. I'm bisexual but I've preferred males throughout my reproductive years. I think I prefer females right now.

When I was growing up, my look was quite androgynous. I was skinny and very flat-chested with narrow hips and a contralto voice. Over the years I've tended to prefer boyishly short hair, but I let it grow a bit when carrying my daughter as I didn't want to look like a pregnant boy.

I went to 13 different grammar schools, so I never learned to fit in. My home life was just as disrupted; many months were spent with relatives or at various boarding schools. There were a few reasons for all of this, none of which really considered what might be best for me. I was a brilliant little chameleon, creating fantastic stories about myself as I went into each new situation, knowing how unlikely it was that anyone would get close enough to know the boring truth. I did well in school because of my Aspie brain. It was easy. I was never so engrossed that I couldn't find some mischief, though, and I often gave my mum, when we were together, reason to correct me with beatings. Other children were an audience. I never felt I belonged. If I could go back in time, I would give myself more love. I would force physical hugs until it was comfortable. Forgiveness for everything should have been first, anyway.

I was undiagnosed throughout my career. Just thought of as weird. I think my Asperger's made me a talented and hardworking employee, though. I always took pride in my work and did my best. Some employers were even understanding of my emotionality.

Later in life I heard about Temple Grandin. After doing my research, I finally took an online test and presented it to the doctor. After a year of therapy with a PhD psychologist I received a casual diagnosis of high-functioning autism. He said he couldn't rule it out, and that I was 'probably autistic'. We agreed that a formal diagnosis would be too expensive and time-consuming to pursue, since there was nothing to be gained at my age in the way of help or financial support.

I went through a few months of bitterness and resentment about this. I accepted the truth of it, but I felt sorry for myself that nobody had ever just accepted me as I am. Nobody had ever just loved me enough to make allowances for my shortcomings which, as it turns out, were no fault of my own. I'd always thought I had some kind of moral deficit. Realizing that I'm autistic has meant a lot of gradual forgiveness and letting go of old resentments. Forgiving myself mostly, but also those who couldn't understand me and my behavior. How could they, when I didn't even know myself? Nowadays, I try not to think about how I come across to other people. I can all too easily fall into that pre-adolescent awkwardness which neurotypicals endure as just a phase.

I'm very shy of the people living nearby, so I tend to avoid encounters if I can. I do better out in the country where people aren't so close to one another. Unfortunately, my life is currently being partially controlled by a close neighbor's electronic pest-repeller. My sensory acuity makes it as annoying for me as it must be for the ants and rats. I think it prevents us all from sleeping. Before the repeller and before the ants and rats, other creatures used to visit. There were rabbits, racoons and possums. They were all a comfort to me, even the skunks. Now only crickets and lizards are bountiful. And the ants and rats, of course. They've acclimatized to the repeller.

Most days, I start the morning by putting my bicycle outside and locking it to a tree. I then feed my pair of doves and my goldfish, Nudie. After coffee, I check Facebook. It's the primary way I keep in touch with my two daughters, one of whom also has Asperger's. My daughters are my greatest source of joy. They are also my greatest source of pain because we are apart and don't really get along. I have two dear friends who I rely heavily upon, but I do most of my socializing online, mostly on Facebook. I think social media is an emotional lifeline for those of us who are fortunate enough to have it. Without Facebook, I think a lot of us would all be like pre-techy Aspies with our noses in books or playing solitary games. Friendship means a great deal to me, but I can be abrasive. My intelligence seems to put people off. I have to constantly edit myself and dumb down; it gets exhausting.

The rest of my day is spent pottering around my little cottage, tending to plants, playing video games, listening to music, watching TV and shows on YouTube. I get around to eating midday sometime when I finally feel hungry. Once my blood sugar is raised, I'll tackle whatever projects I might have going, like Christmas or birthday presents I need to make or order for my daughter's little family. Bathing and attending to personal general hygiene routines depend upon the day's social expectations. If I expect to be alone, it depends upon if I offend myself yet. I also attend to chores like laundry and watering the plants. I do clean the house, but it usually looks quite messy.

I try to eat a proper meal in the evening and remember to take my antipsychotic medication. It's supposed to help me cope with the ultralow frequency vibrations from the repeller – vibrations I must endure because nobody else can hear or feel them like me and the other pests. I then take a couple more sleeping pills before hopefully drifting off to sleep.

Since the arrival of the repeller, a large portion of my attention has been consumed by dealing with it. It's become a nightmare as other people who lack my sensitivity assume that I'm hallucinating or delirious. Before the repeller arrived, my thoughts were either about my girls or my physical challenges such as pain management for arthritis and other typical age-related joint problems. I also have mild Ehlers-Danlos syndrome. It means I have soft joints and connective tissues. I am fortunate that my special interests, like herbalism, decrease the impact of my elderly health issues. Kitchen magic, chemistry, medicine and cooking, herbs, including cannabis and whatever else

I can grow. Living things are what I've always enjoyed most, pets and plants. Unfortunately, I'm unable to have pets here and it's getting too difficult to look after my plants. I have to cut back. I'm getting very enthusiastic about politics these days, so maybe I'll swap my current interests for this instead. I may even get tempted to march. Not likely, but I envision it!

Out in the wider world today, I see all the awareness and help that there is for kids with autism. There's nothing, though, for seniors like me who've struggled and repeatedly failed to do more than merely survive, even though they're gifted. Over time, I've become more objective about my own behavior. I now recognize my tendency to sometimes catastrophize and take situations or trials to be life-threatening or at least more taxing and injurious than they really are. I now worry, though, that when in the care of others, I will be disregarded and not taken seriously when I fear something is wrong. I'm afraid of being thought of as crazy, when in fact I'm perfectly sane. It's just that my experience is different, more intense than my neurotypical counterparts. I worry about abuse and confinement. It's happening already.

Michael

Systematist

Getting my notice of induction into the armed forces of the United States had, from the standpoint of an autistic kid who had little idea of how human social systems operate, been a total nightmare. It was 1968 and I didn't expect to react well to the onset of combat. I anticipated falling apart completely. In actual fact, I became intensely focused on the situation, despite the intense sensory overload. I endured many stressful situations, but I found myself collected, rational and effective. By the time I left the system in 1971, I found that few challenges could compete with what I had met and overcome.

I'm now a balding, slightly paunchy old guy, with a short white beard who often walks with a cane. I dabbled in religion with varying degrees of intensity up until 1985. Since then I've been what you might call a primitive Buddhist.

My LGBTQ+ rainbow letter is 'B', but I'm in the 50th year of a faithful and monogamous heterosexual marriage. We're not entirely sure how it all happened, but we seem to tolerate each other reasonably well. My wife is not autistic, but she's not neurotypical either. We live in a fast-growing community north of Dallas, Texas. We've been here now for 25 years, on and off, but we're planning to move soon to be closer to the offspring.

I'm currently semi-retired as my wonderful place of work have cut me a deal where I only need to be available for two hours a day. This means I can be the highly qualified expert they need without the financial burden of keeping me on full-time as, essentially, a shoe store clerk. The company is 'virtual', i.e. everyone works remotely. At my age, the Social Security system (for the time being at least) makes up for the loss of income.

My routine nowadays is as follows. I arise at 6.30am, go downstairs to feed the cats, make myself a cup of tea on the way. After pottering about for a bit, I then have a brutal 22-foot commute to my workspace, ready to start at 8.30. I fire up the lovely computer system my work provided, check email, chat with colleagues who have questions and attend telephone/video conference calls, etc. When that's all done, I may wander off and feed the cats again, fuss about with Facebook. If they need me for anything else, the Director of Operations will send me a text.

The company I work for manufactures software products that people can use to send large amounts of email to a (hopefully) receptive audience. My job involves analyzing problems that customers may have getting their emails delivered to people's inboxes. I started in this sector 23 years ago with what I now recognize as an autistic special interest: email spam as a pathological outgrowth of the availability of a worldwide communications revolution.

My daily thoughts always include the fixations and suicidal ideation that accompanies my depression. It's mostly all just a familiar nuisance. It was back in 1987 that I learned that the DSM III (*Diagnostic and Statistical Manual*, Third Edition) stated that children could be clinically depressed. This discovery meant that my life experiences suddenly had a coherent explanation. I was duly told by a variety of professionals that my maladies were 'progressive and degenerative'. It's turned out to be an accurate forecast.

I've always enjoyed learning about formally diagnosed neurological issues, as well as engaging in discussions on Facebook with support groups for those who are affected. It was after a number of exchanges about life experiences on one such page that someone said, 'You do realize you're autistic, right?' That set off a whole new voyage of discovery. I realized that while autistic people are often invisible to others, they're also often invisible to themselves.

Since learning about autism (mine and anybody else's) at age 68, it has become a special interest with the same intensity that email spam was a couple of decades back. I spend a lot of time reading and pondering how human cognitive and behavioral systems might be structured to exhibit the manifestations of autism. I'm revising my notions about the future.

One thing I've come to realize is that there are primary cultural differences between the autism community and the autistic community. My attempts at participating in (or even understanding) the community of parents and vendors of treatments and interventions has been marginal to say the least. Instead, I've gravitated naturally to what appears to me to be the mainstream community of autistic adults. In doing so, I have gained a large array of fascinating friends.

Just a few months after realizing I was autistic, I was at a weekly wine-tasting session held a short distance from the Microsoft campus in Redmond, Washington. A quite majestic woman joined the tasters; she was looking for some wines to celebrate her wedding anniversary. Seeing her company badge, I knew we were both in the tech sector. We began to discuss the things in the workplace that drove us nuts. We both sensed a pattern in the trend of the discussion and eventually she said, 'OK, you're autistic too, right?' That was definitely one of those 'I've finally found my tribe' moments.

Niboroo

Health Warrior

At ten years old, I was present at the suicide of my stepfather. Being autistic stopped me getting to my feelings. It took many years for me to be able to relay the story; it came out with a strange sort of laughter. Suppressing it for so long still affects me when watching a movie or TV depiction of someone starting to kill themselves; I can't help but close up and look away.

I'm an explorer, an adventurer, a modern-day Renaissance woman. I'm always curious; I was born this way – oodles of things fascinate me. I enjoy reading biographies, autobiographies, astronomy, history, cultural behaviours, the workings of the human body. It was the latter fascination that led to a long and successful career in pain management.

Throughout my life, I've had a tendency to follow wishes and instinct, rather than making plans. Unfortunately, this has meant feeling trapped within decisions that did not feel fully mine. It's also meant dealing with the long-term consequences. Marriage, for example. I remember body signals that I couldn't interpret, shaking uncontrollably during the first part of the ceremony. Fourteen years later, I discovered the lesbian within.

I was diagnosed in my mid-70s. I'm in my 80s now. I live in a senior community apartment where my cat used to live as well. Unfortunately, I lost her just a few days ago. The apartment is within a small town with a university nearby. I keep a small garden going on my small porch so that I can eat fresh lettuces, mint, chives, parsley, and I love smelling the jasmine vines when they bloom.

I'm most at home in the natural world with animals. I can trust them to be real. They nurture me so much more than people ever have. Art nurtures me too – dance, music, athletics, crafts, photography, poetry, writing. I like staying up late to be alone with the quiet. I write and do so with my earplugs in place. They make it so much easier to listen to myself!

My deepest and most probing thoughts come just after I wake. I leave time for them – hours if need be – in bed where I feel most at peace. My unguarded brain is very susceptible to the intrusion of other energies that are not my own. They sneak in when I'm just about to sleep or just coming out of a dream. I have learned to reject them and verbally tell them to get lost. Which they do!

It's important for me to get out almost every day, to get beyond my purposefully single, solitary life. My shul is close by; I've been active there for 18 years, feeling more at home there than anywhere else. I'm not lonely but I do miss my daughters and granddaughters. They're all extremely busy and live far away, so I seldom see them.

I make sure to keep the few appointments that I make. They're always in the afternoon. Sometimes I combine them with shopping or seeing a movie. Sometimes I meet new people when I'm out and about. On occasion I have very good conversations where I feel that I am truly myself, that I'm not having to live up to some pre-formed expectation.

People tend to think I'm at least 20 years younger than I am. Unfortunately, that's not always how I feel. This complicates me internally; I have to act the age I look. I can do this most of the time, but when I can't, I tend to hide myself away. I understand that this is a result of trying to act neurotypical, a put-on that has made me distant from my own real self for many decades.

Since my diagnosis, I've slowly come to identify the toxic people and situations around me, to avoid them as much as possible. I enjoy the company of those who have done their homework, the harder inside work of looking and dealing with their deeper selves, their willingness to keep on growing. I've been in therapy for 15 years. With a therapist who listens beautifully and pays real attention. The therapy helps me live among this small community of age peers. We've all been through the intensity and challenge of coming to live in low-income housing by necessity.

My concerns about my future and being an Aspie are tied in with wanting to live here as I am now for as long as possible. I need to keep on being fit and healthy enough to stay.

I've often heard that people with Asperger's tend not to be athletic. I don't think that's true. We are all individuals, just like the rest of society. I've survived cancer and I've survived Lyme disease. I've got four new joints and I've completed triathlons (16 of them in my 50s). I know the athletic strength and endurance that I'm capable of; I've just got to keep it up.

If I had to be in even a decent nursing home, I think I'd disappear. I'm too free a spirit to be ruled by others or an institution; my senses are too sensitive. I like the quiet order here.

It'd be a huge struggle to make new friends without a lot of inner tension.

My ambition now is to declutter my life, to concentrate on looking after myself. I also want to help others do the same. I believe that self-knowledge makes people kinder to themselves and to others. This new generation of activists inspires me with their passion for righting wrongs. Nowadays, I'm feeling more and more overwhelmed with all I feel I need to do to simplify my life before I leave the planet. I see my moving on not as an end, though, more as my next unknown adventure.